筆尖美學

MODERN CALLIGRAPHY

習字簿

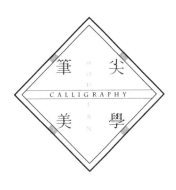

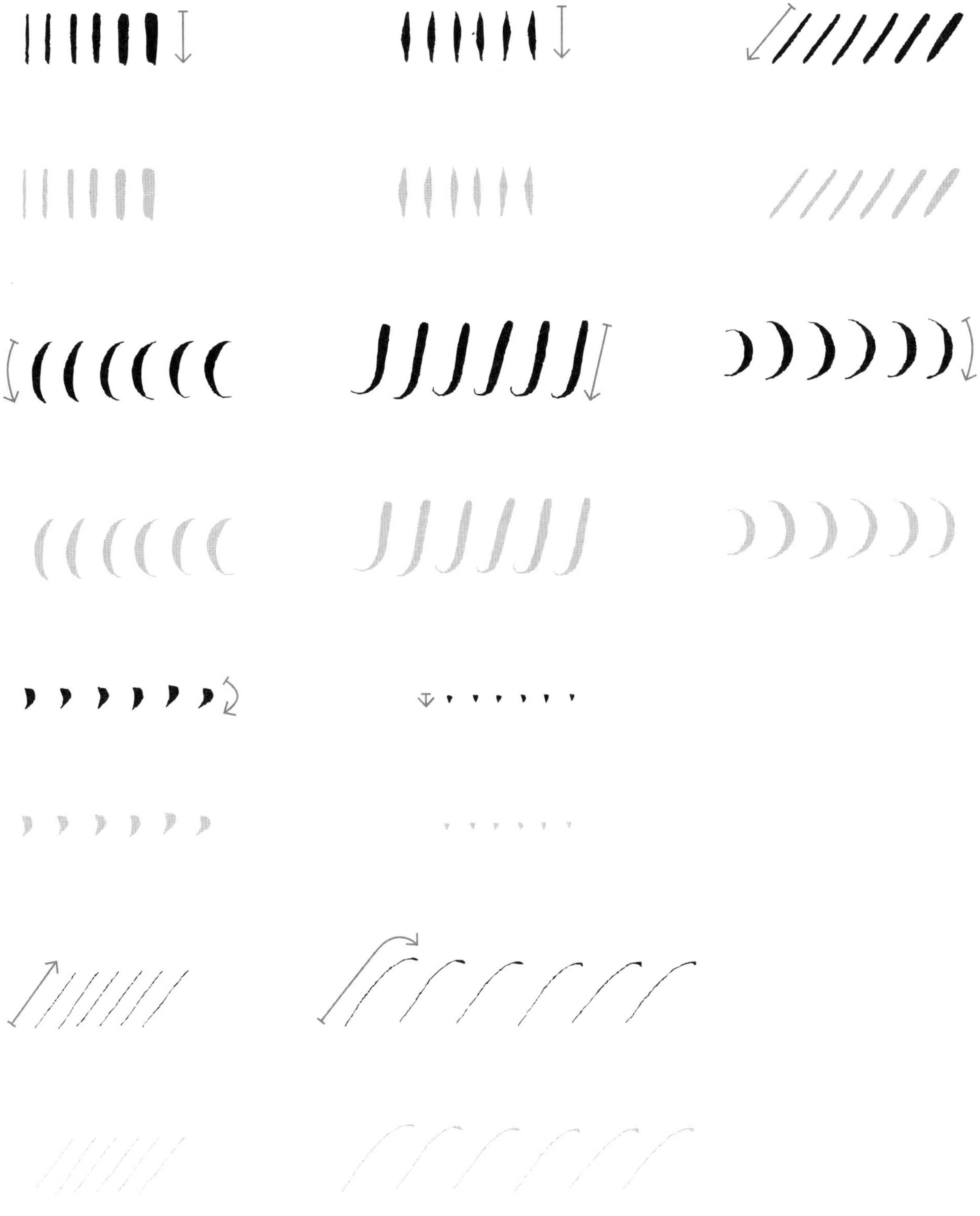

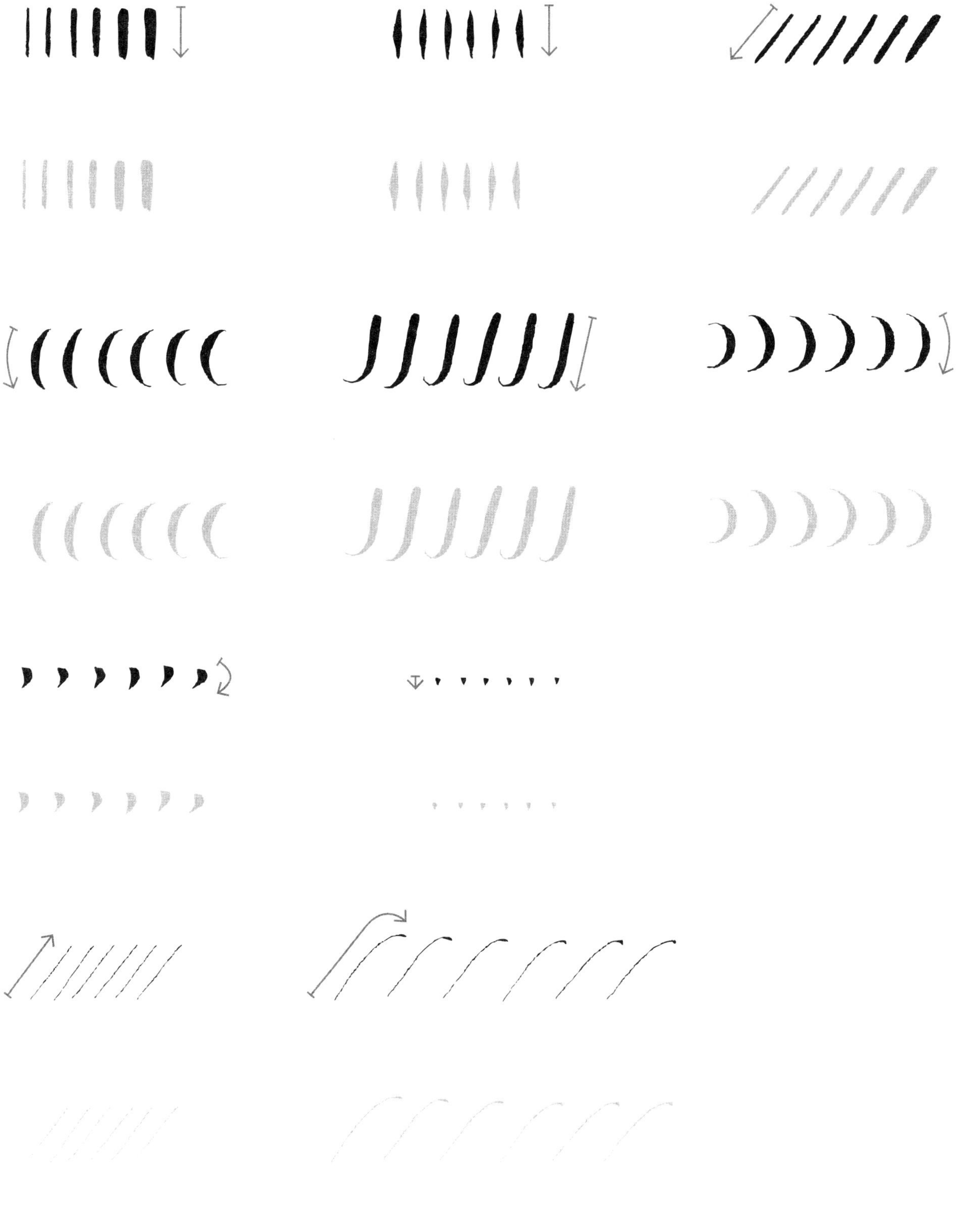

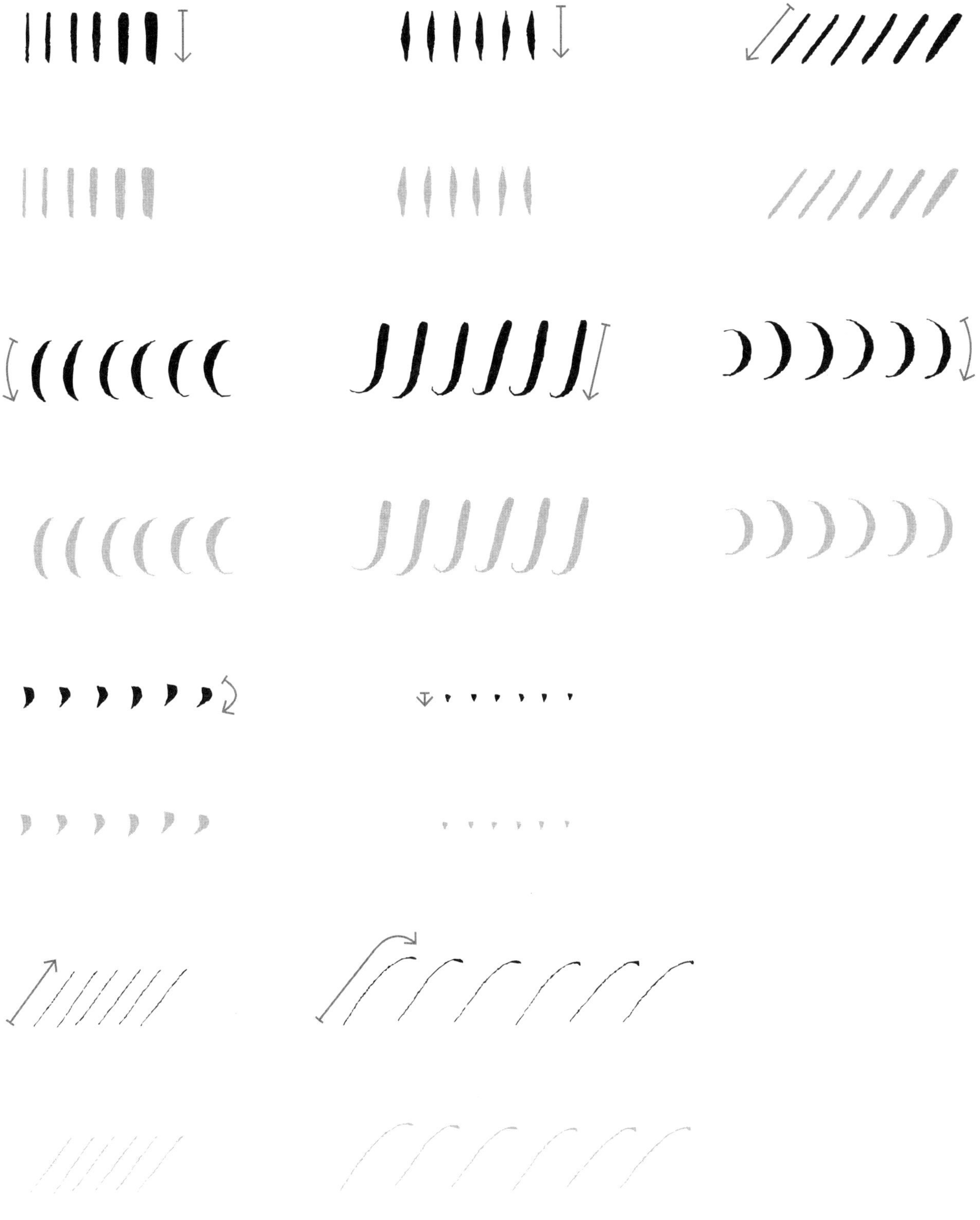

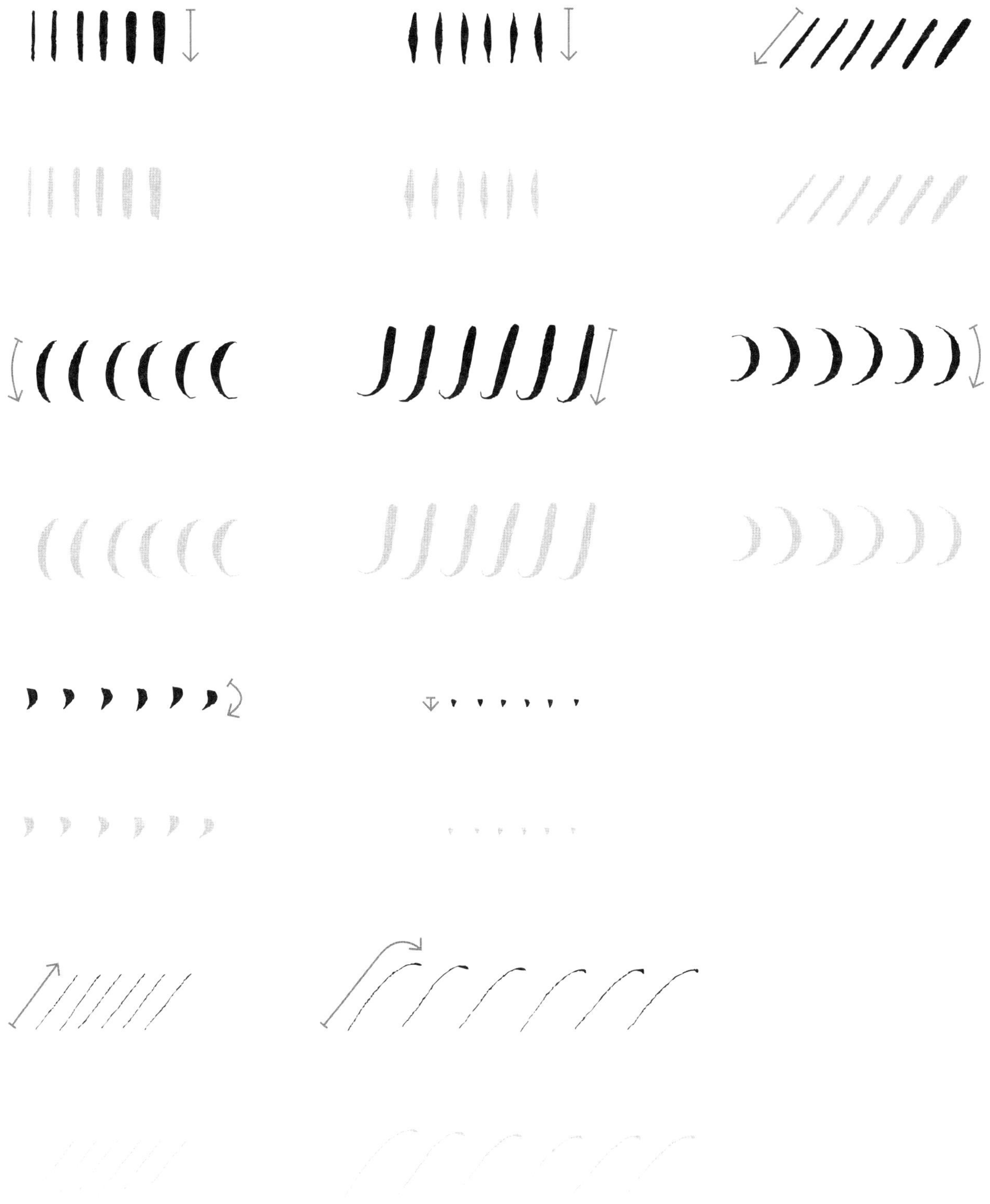

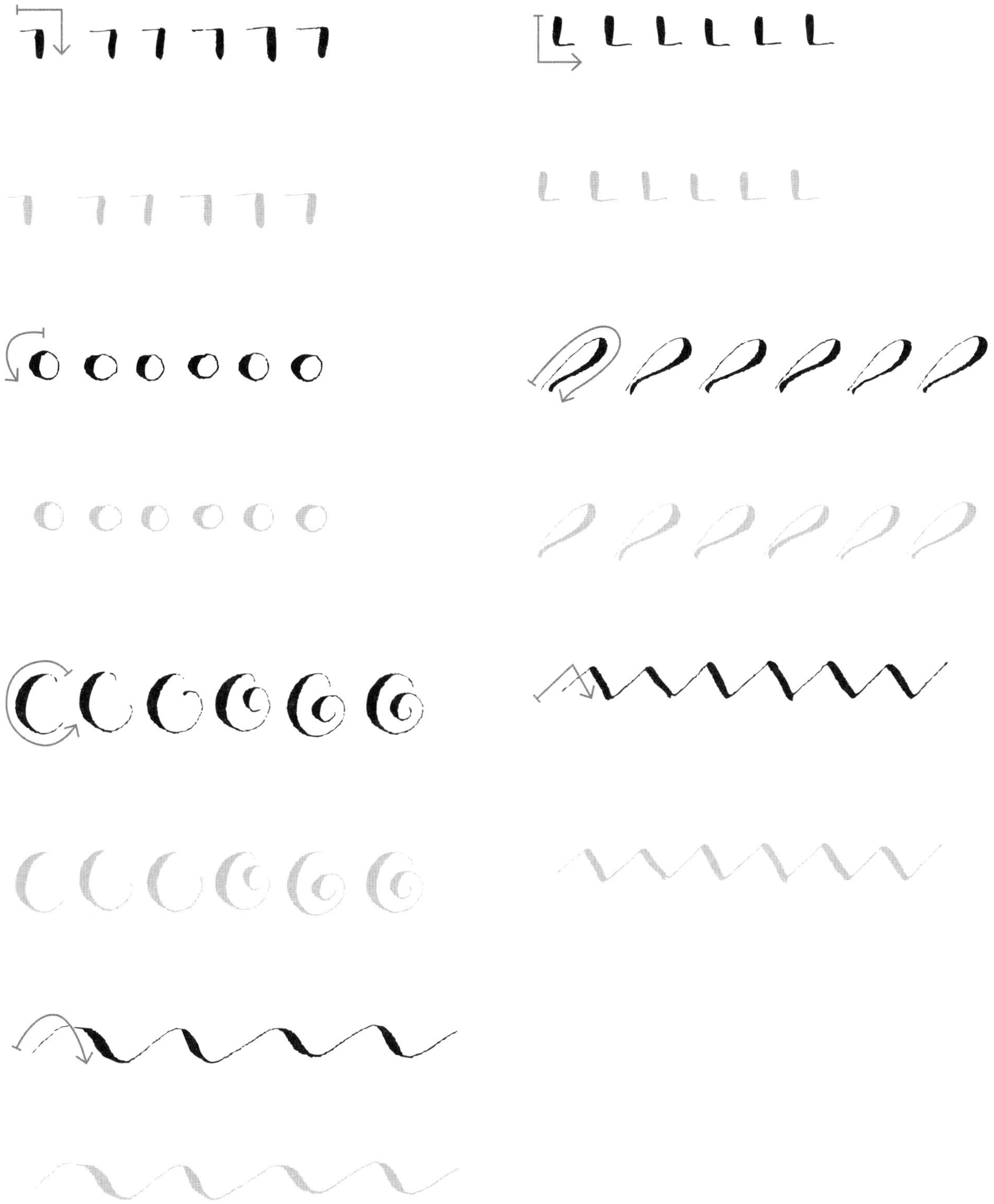

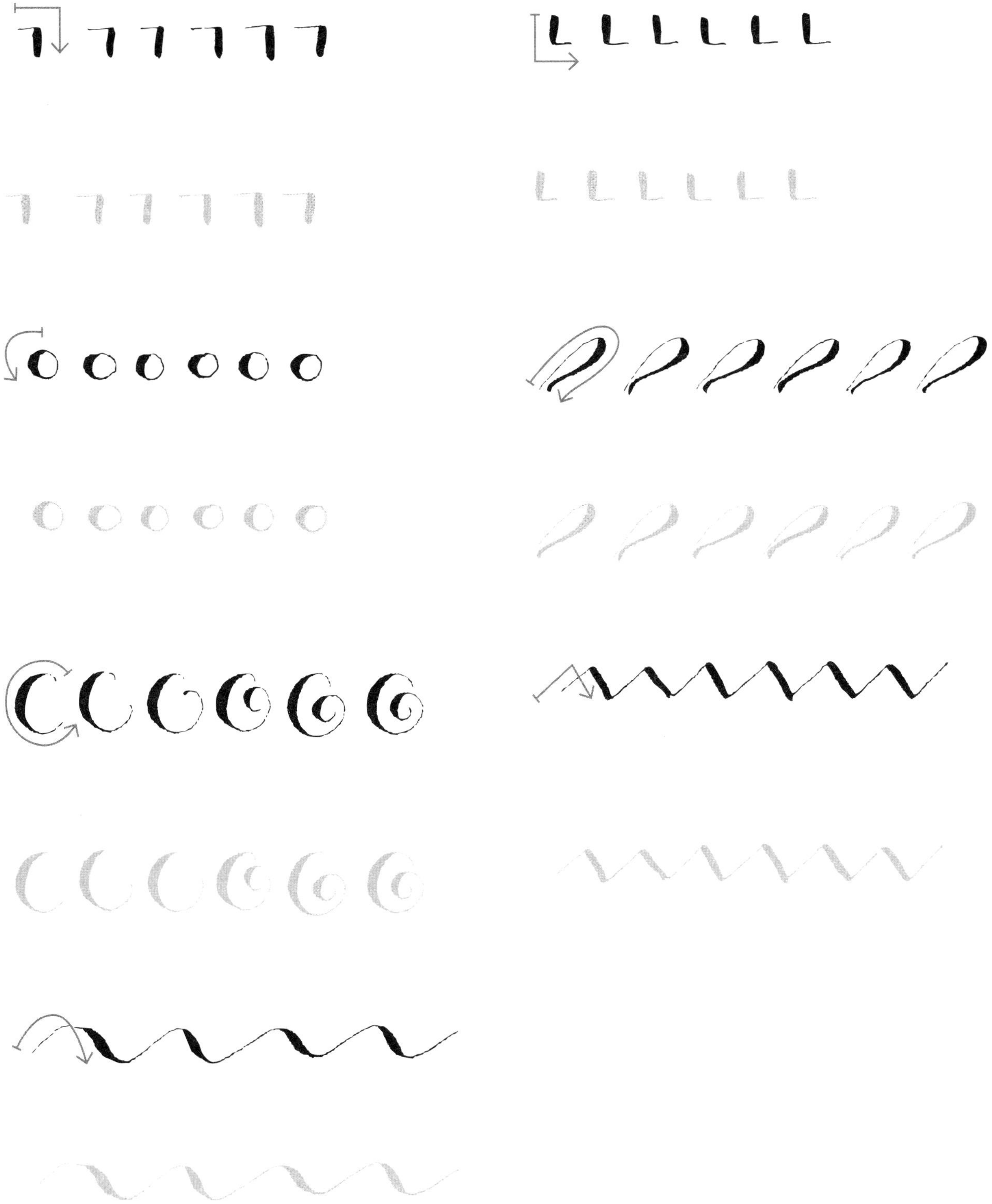

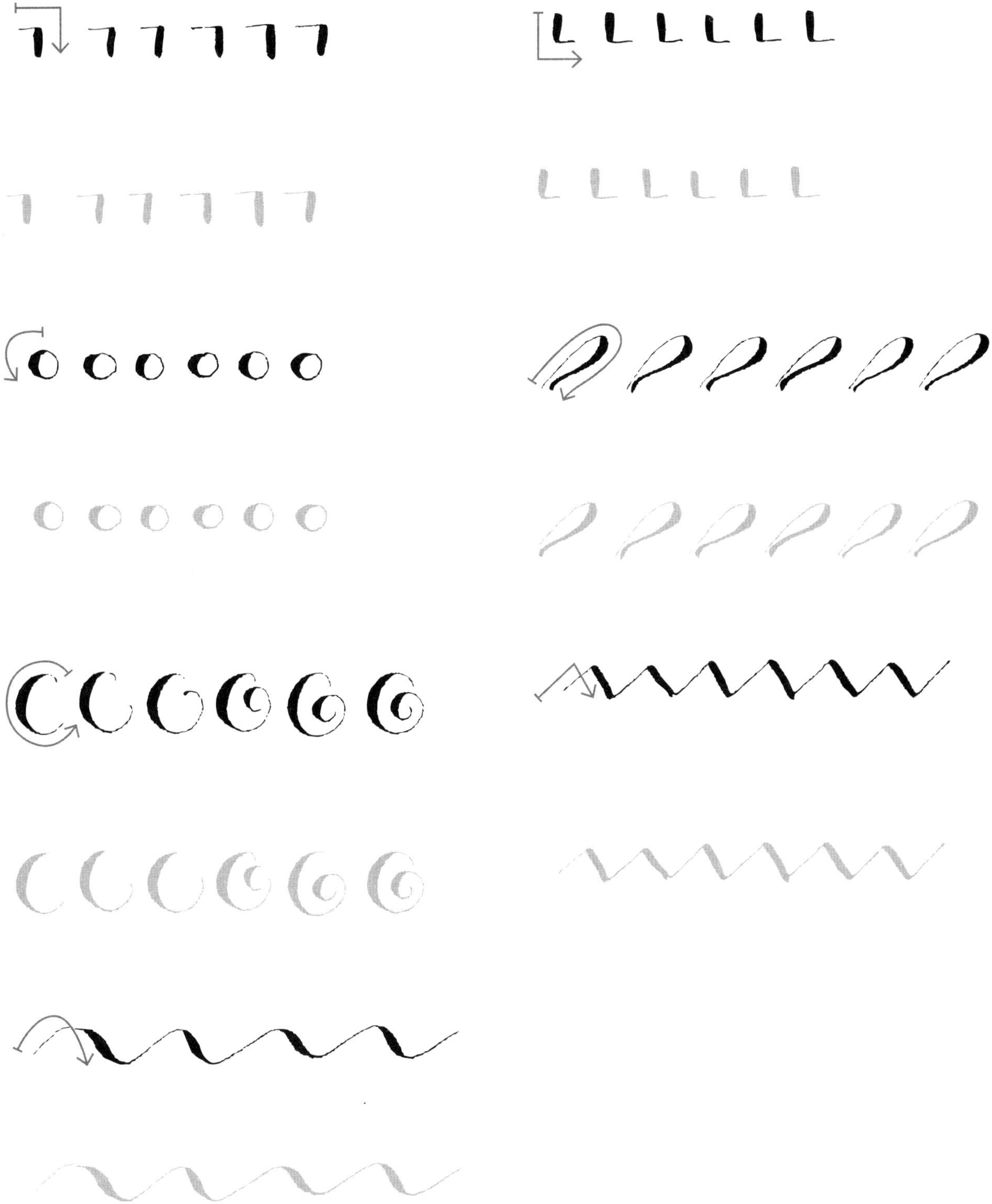

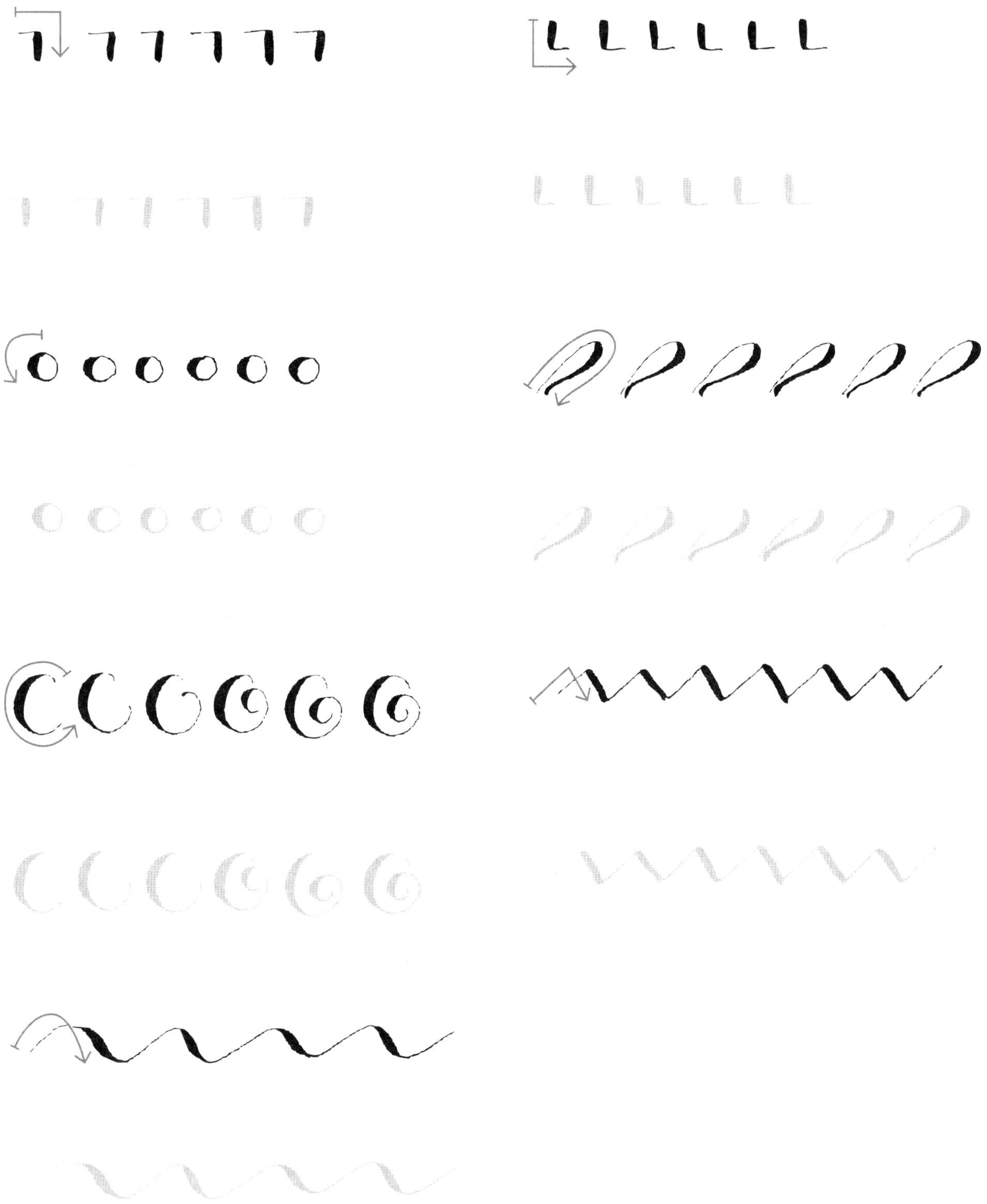

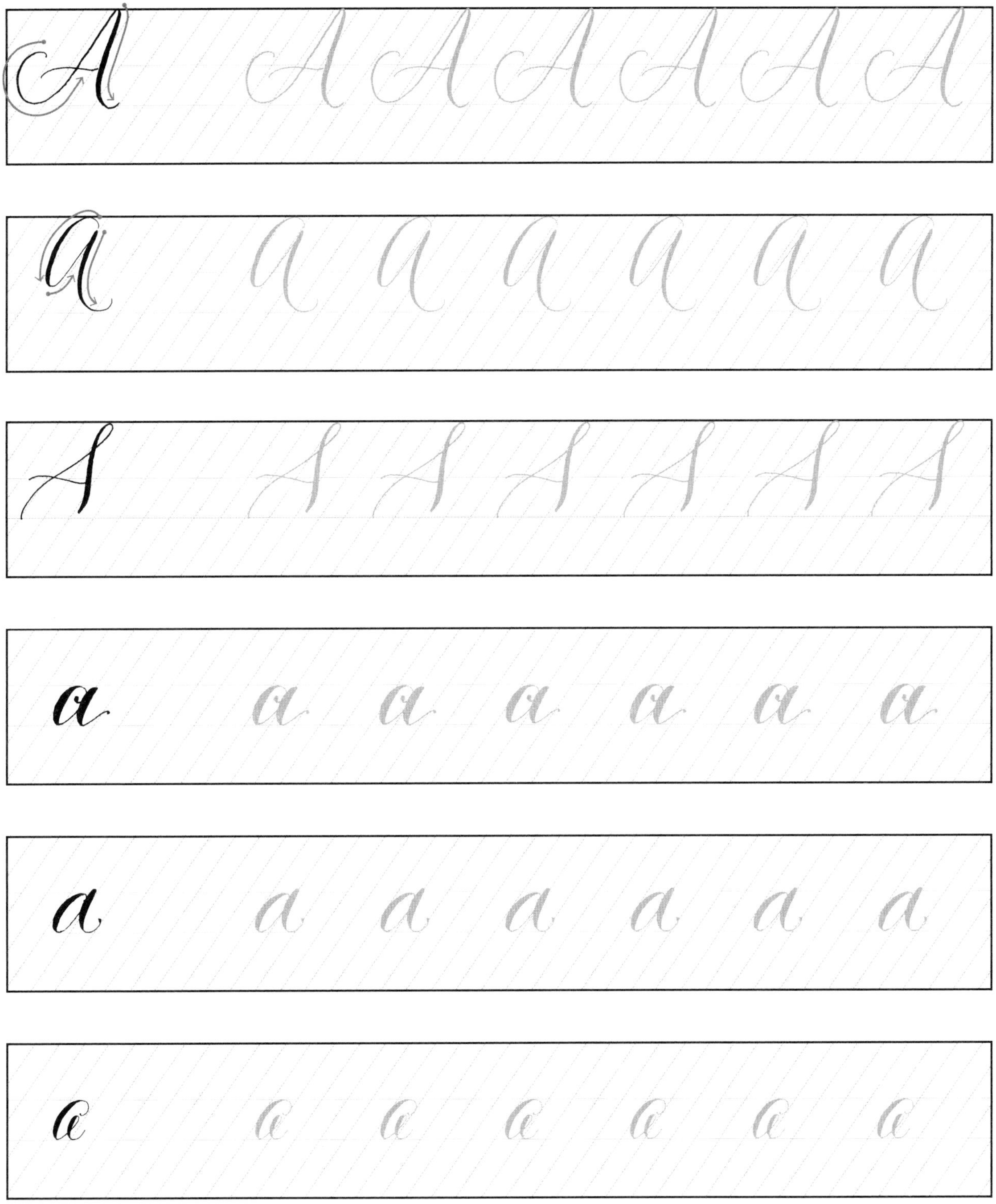

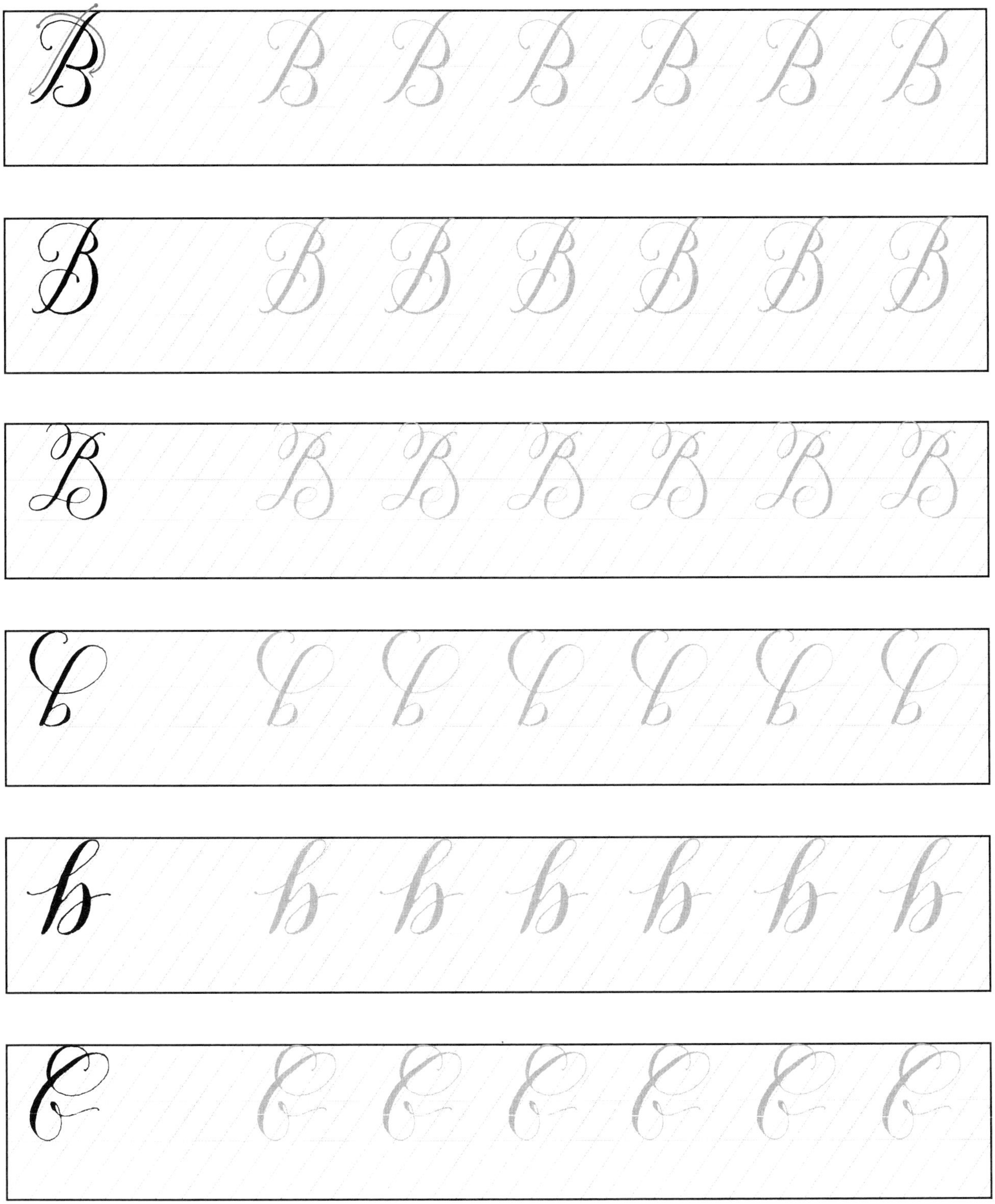

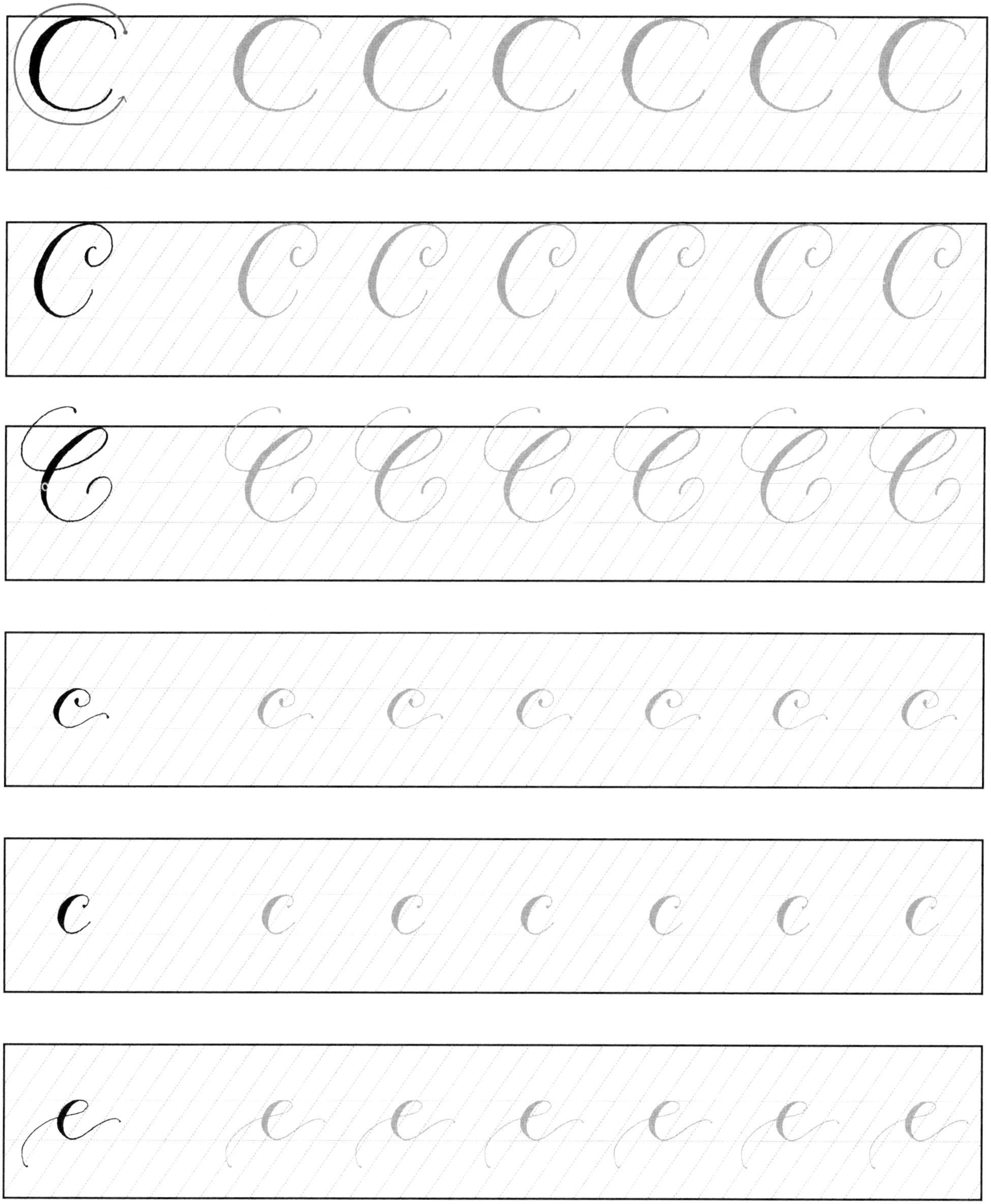

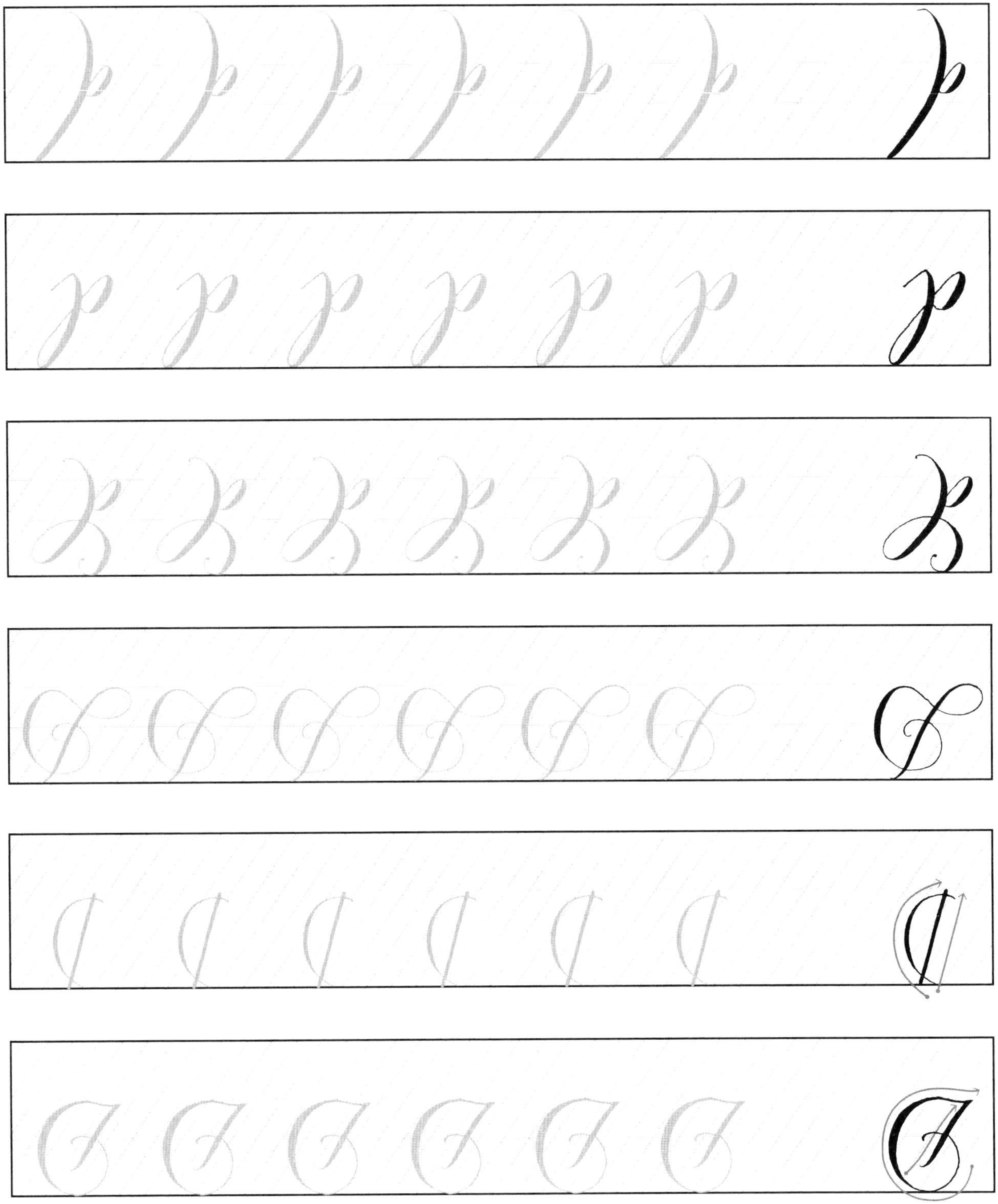

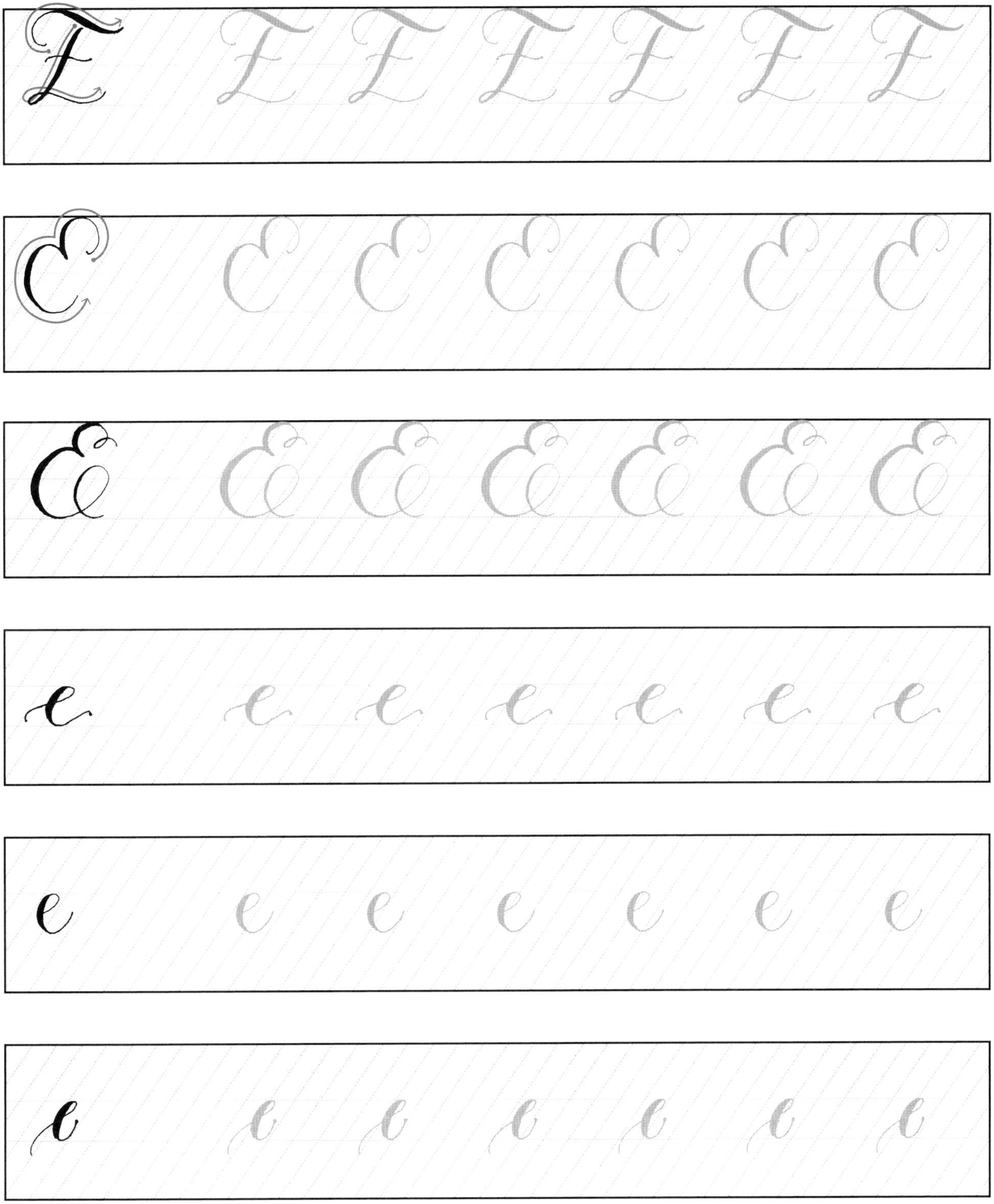

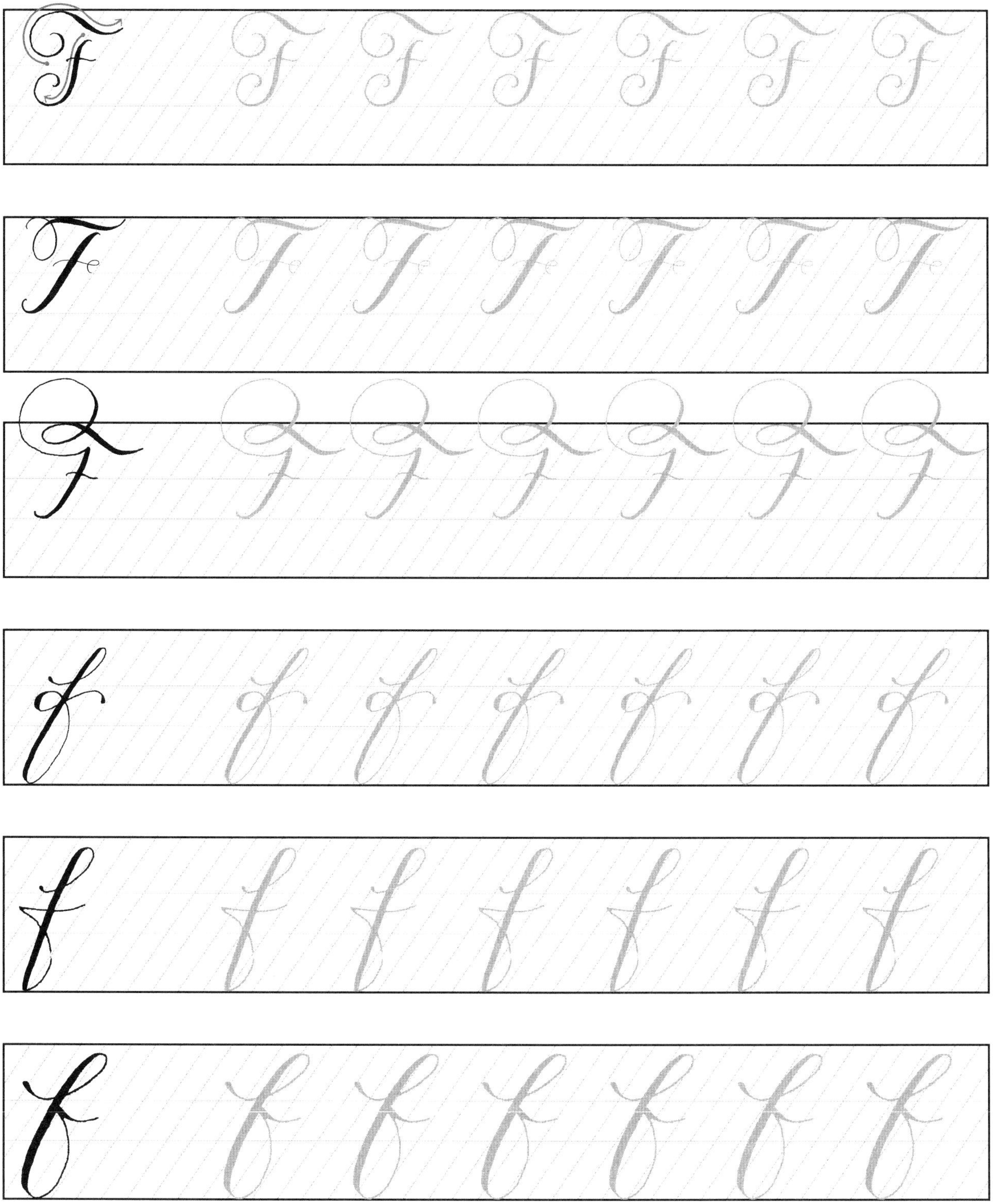

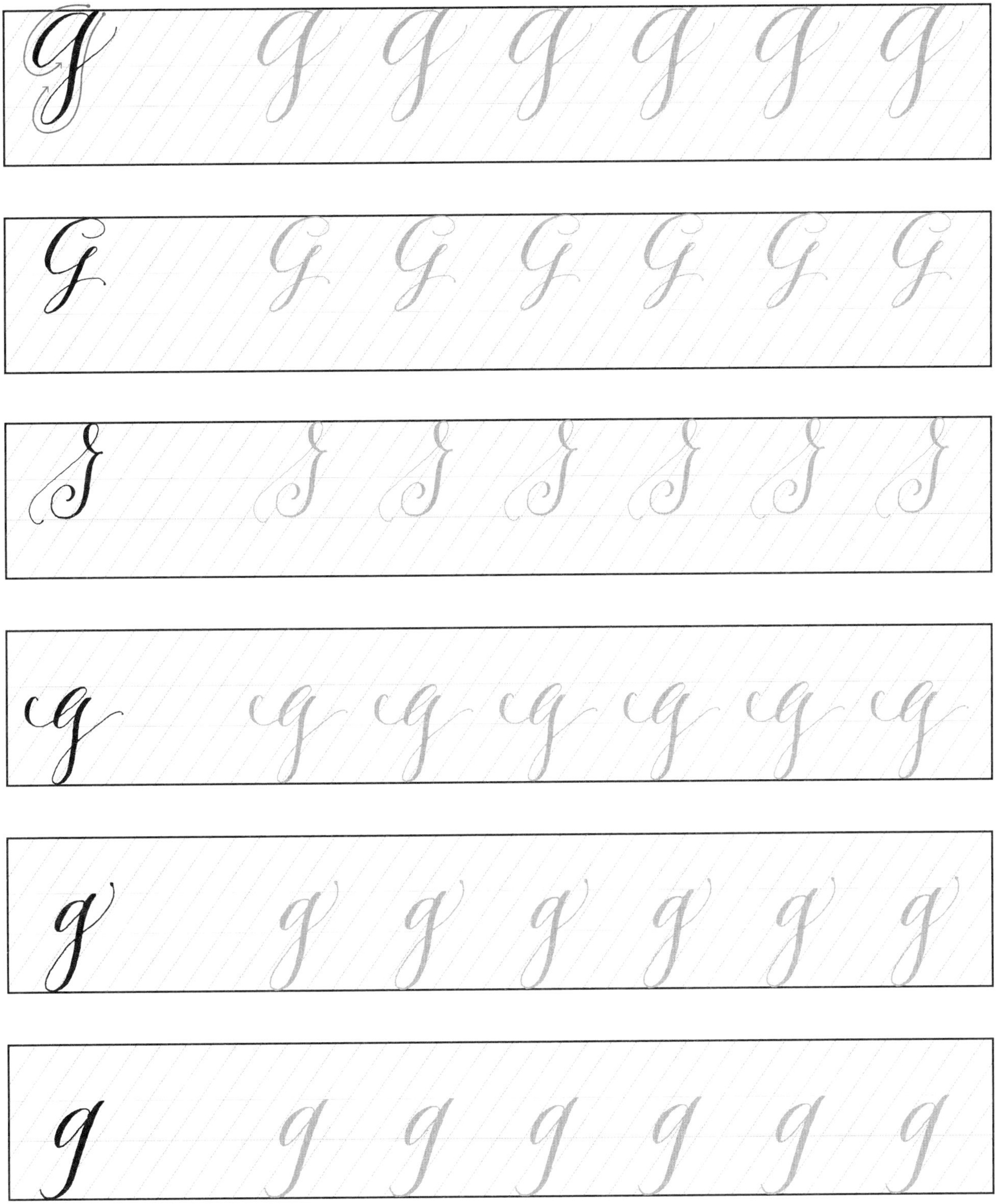

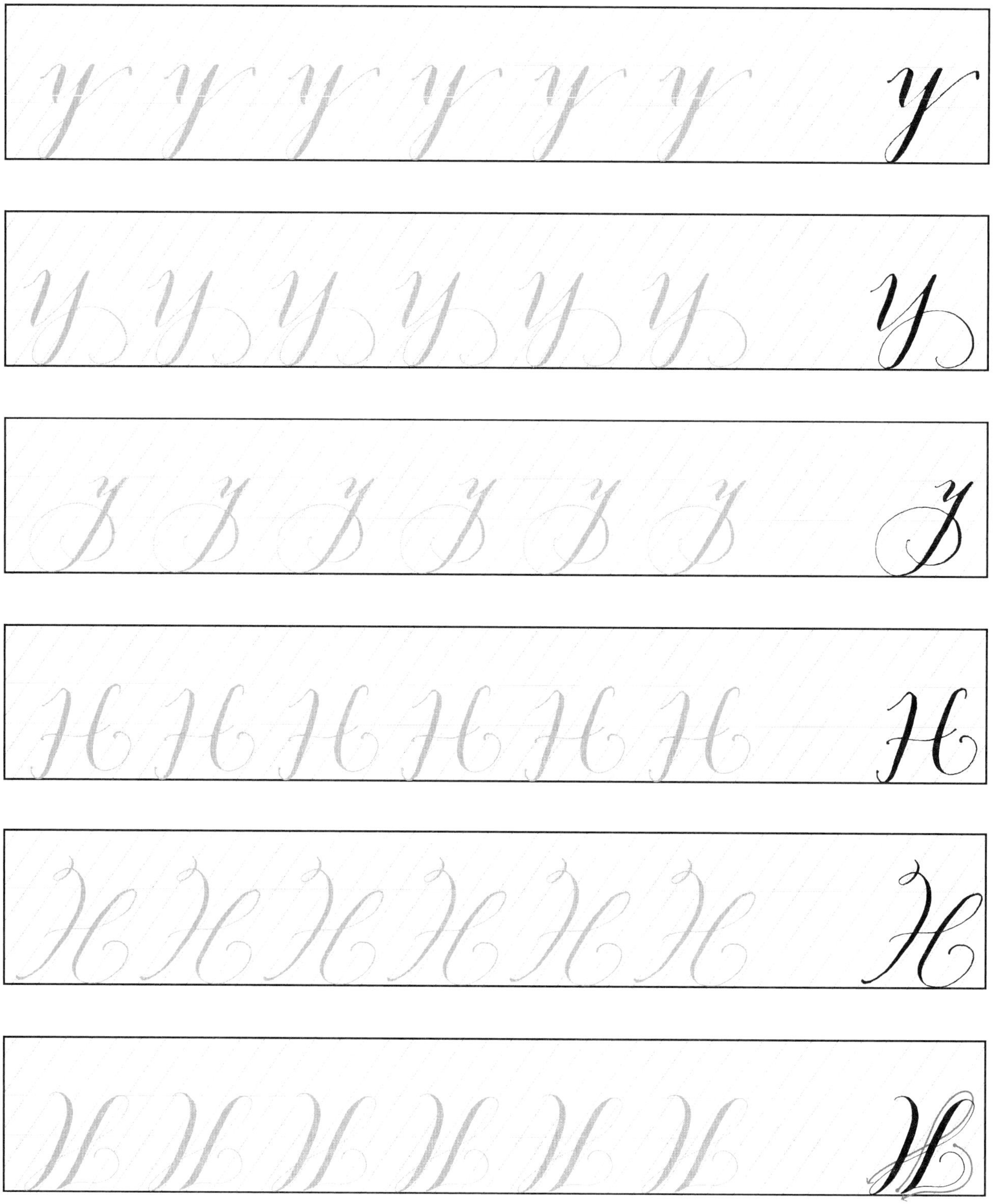

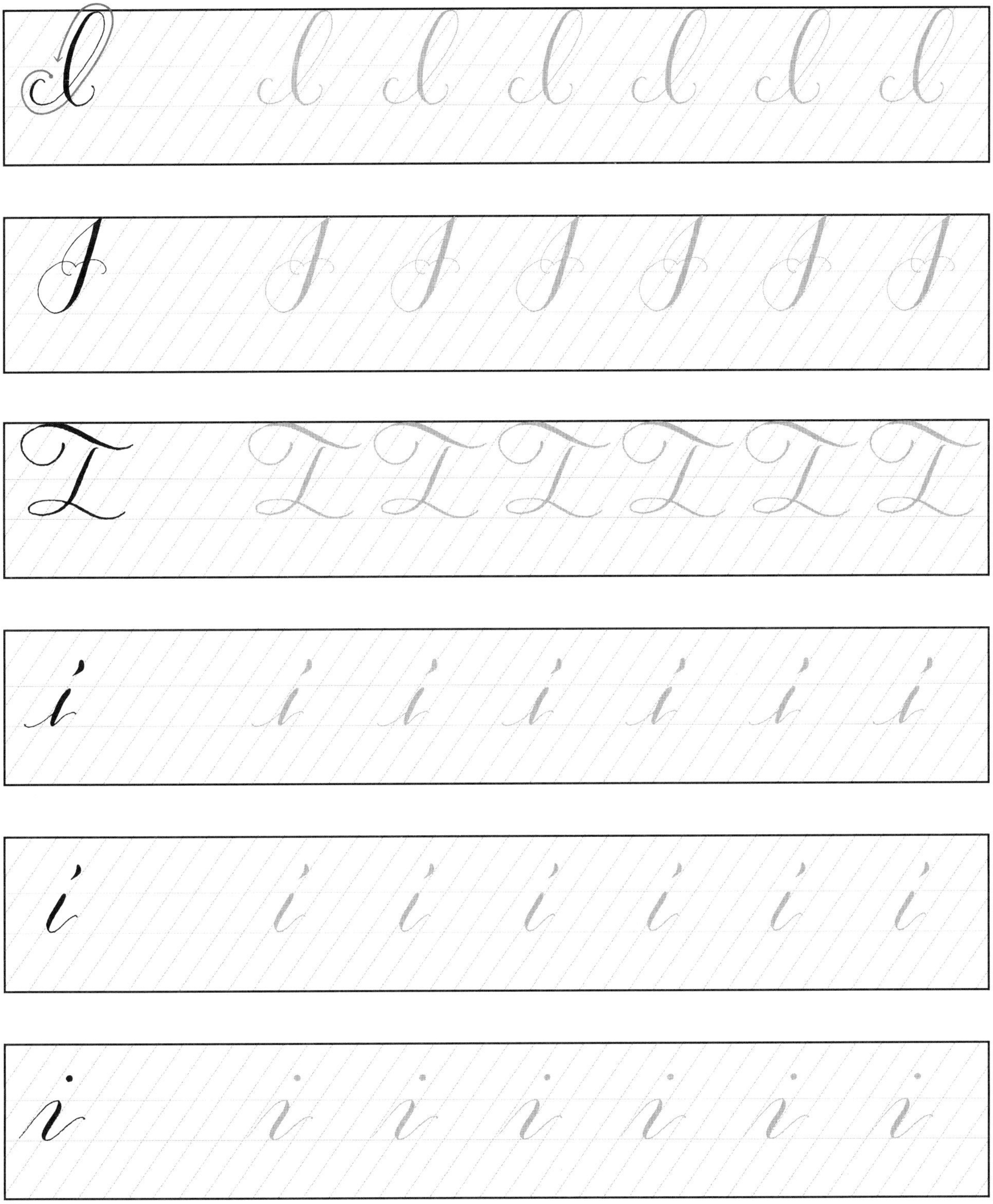

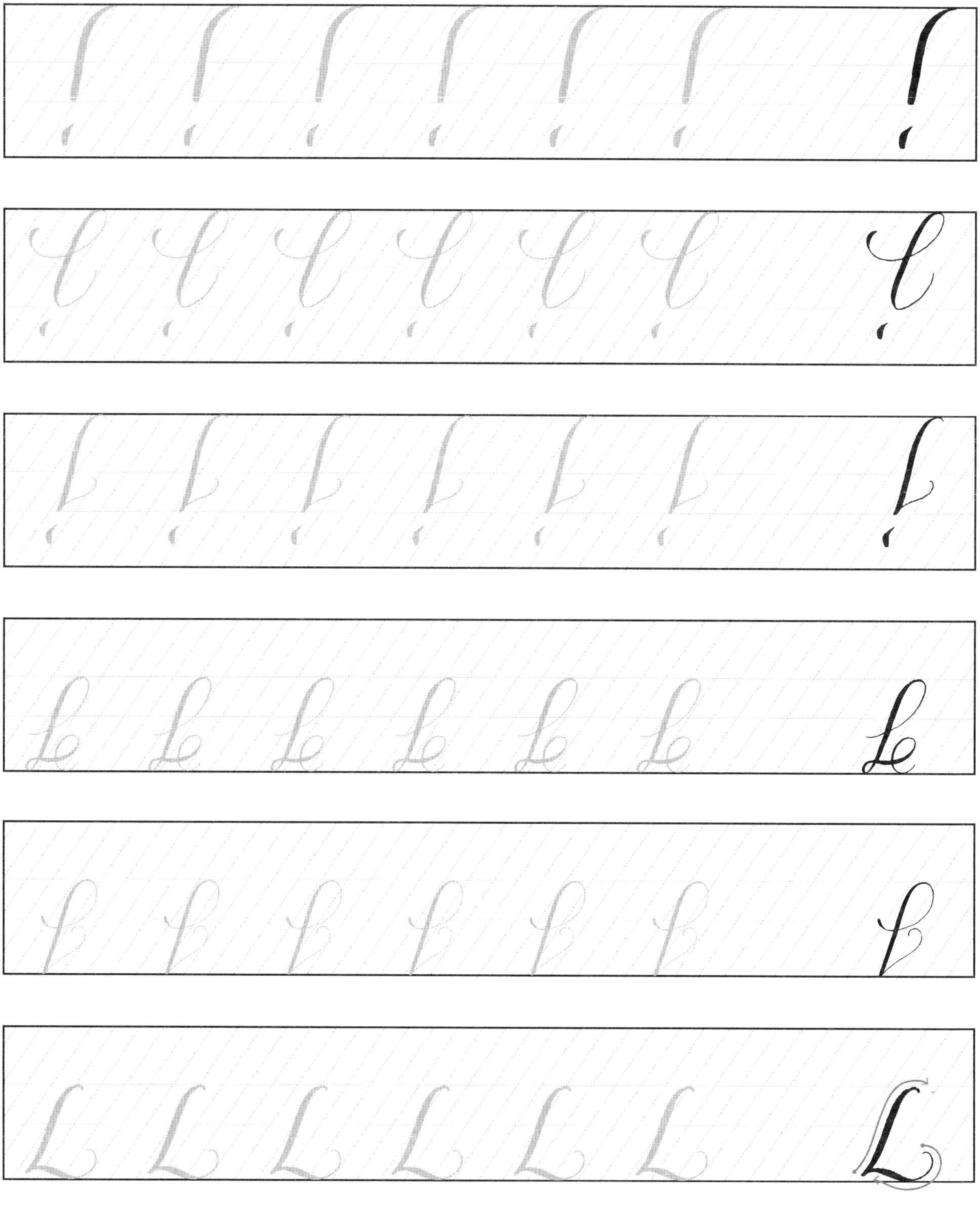

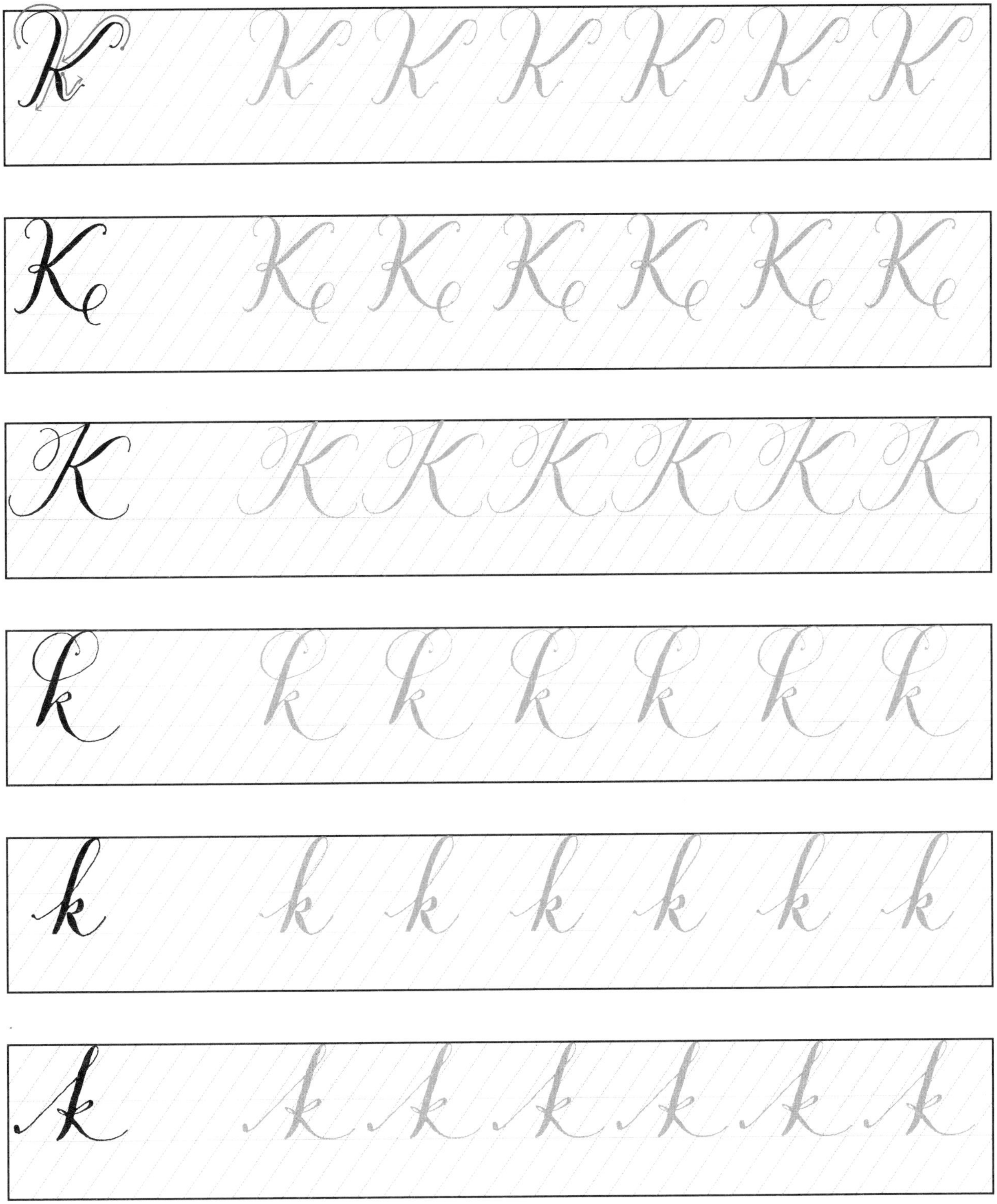

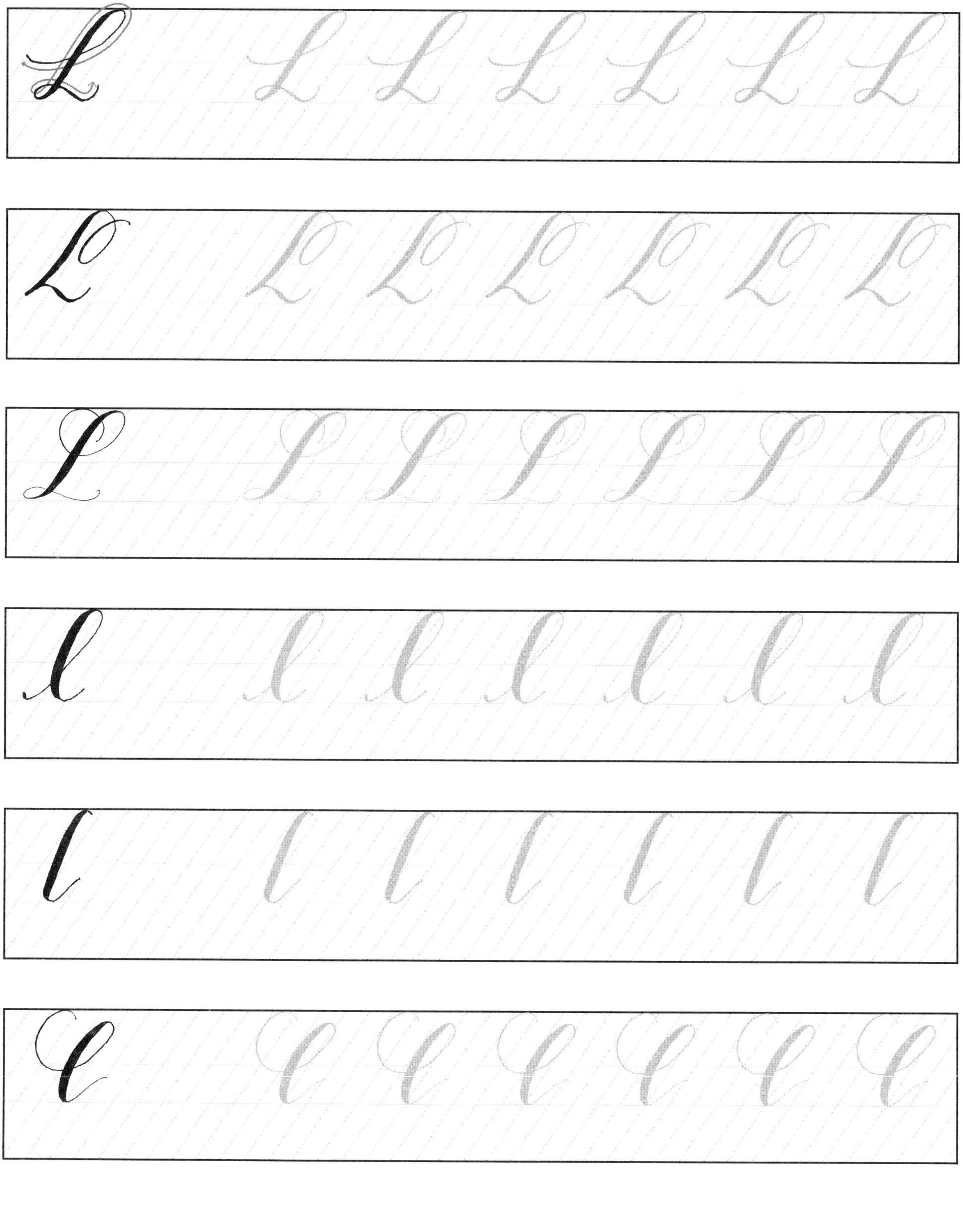

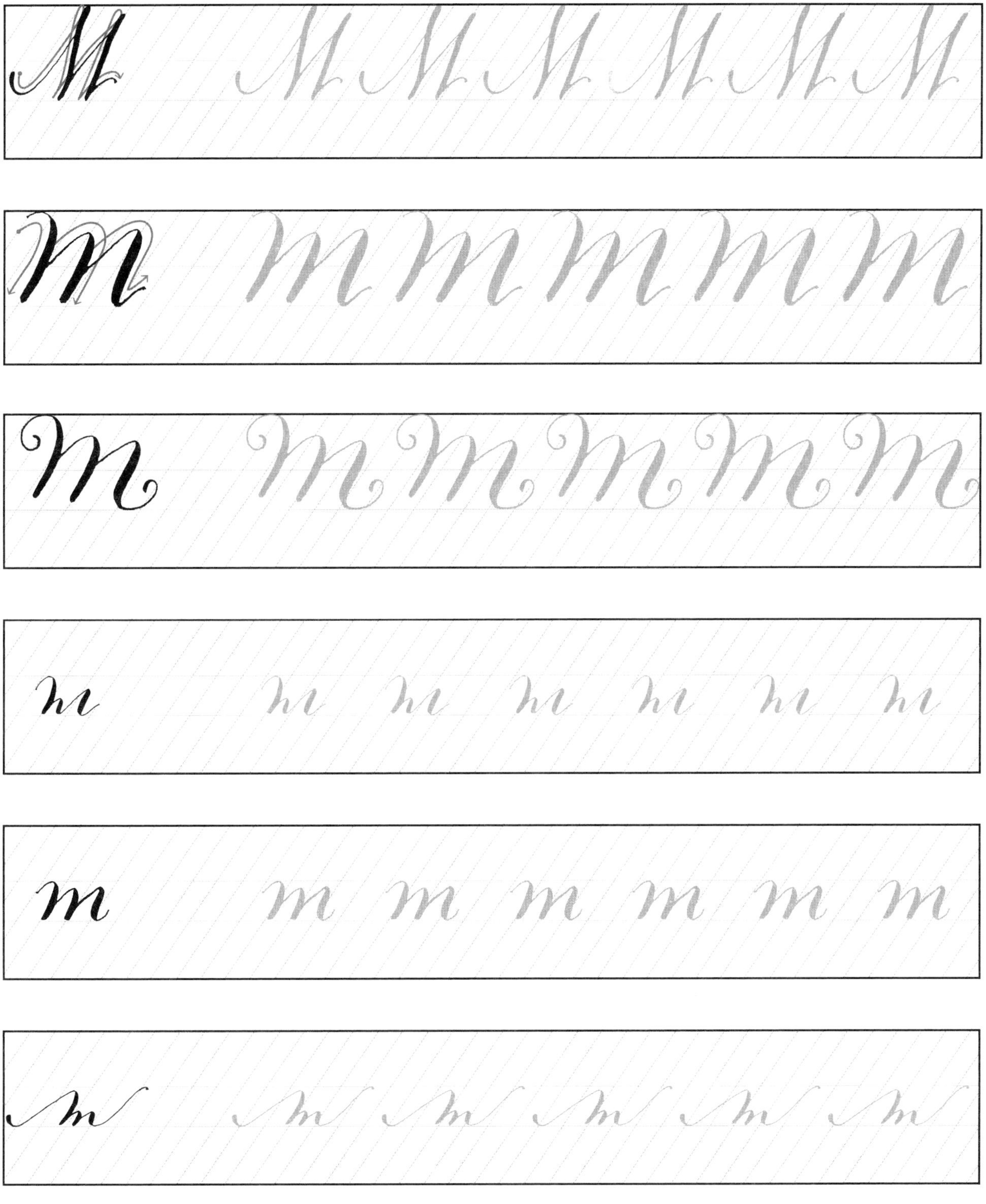

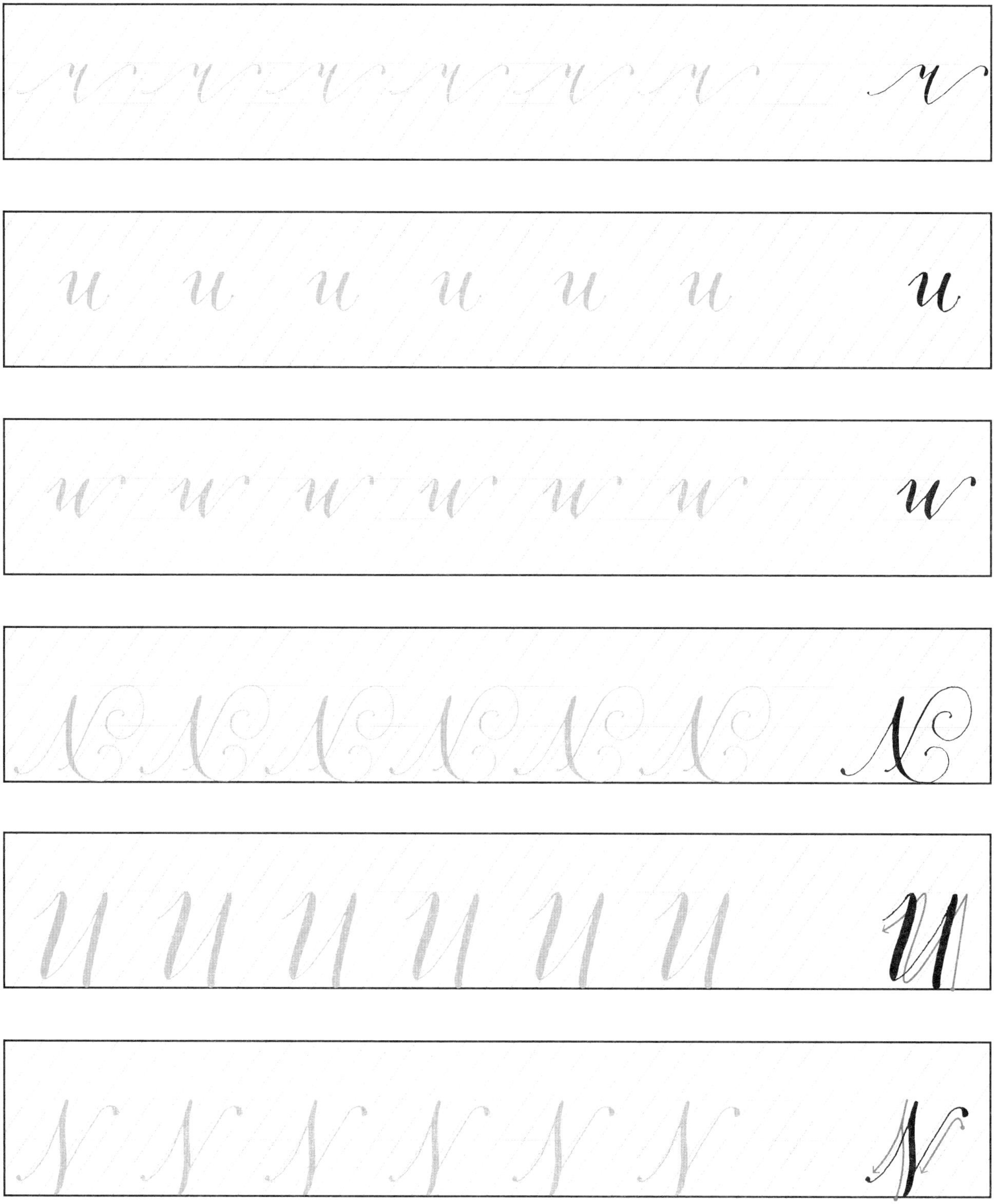

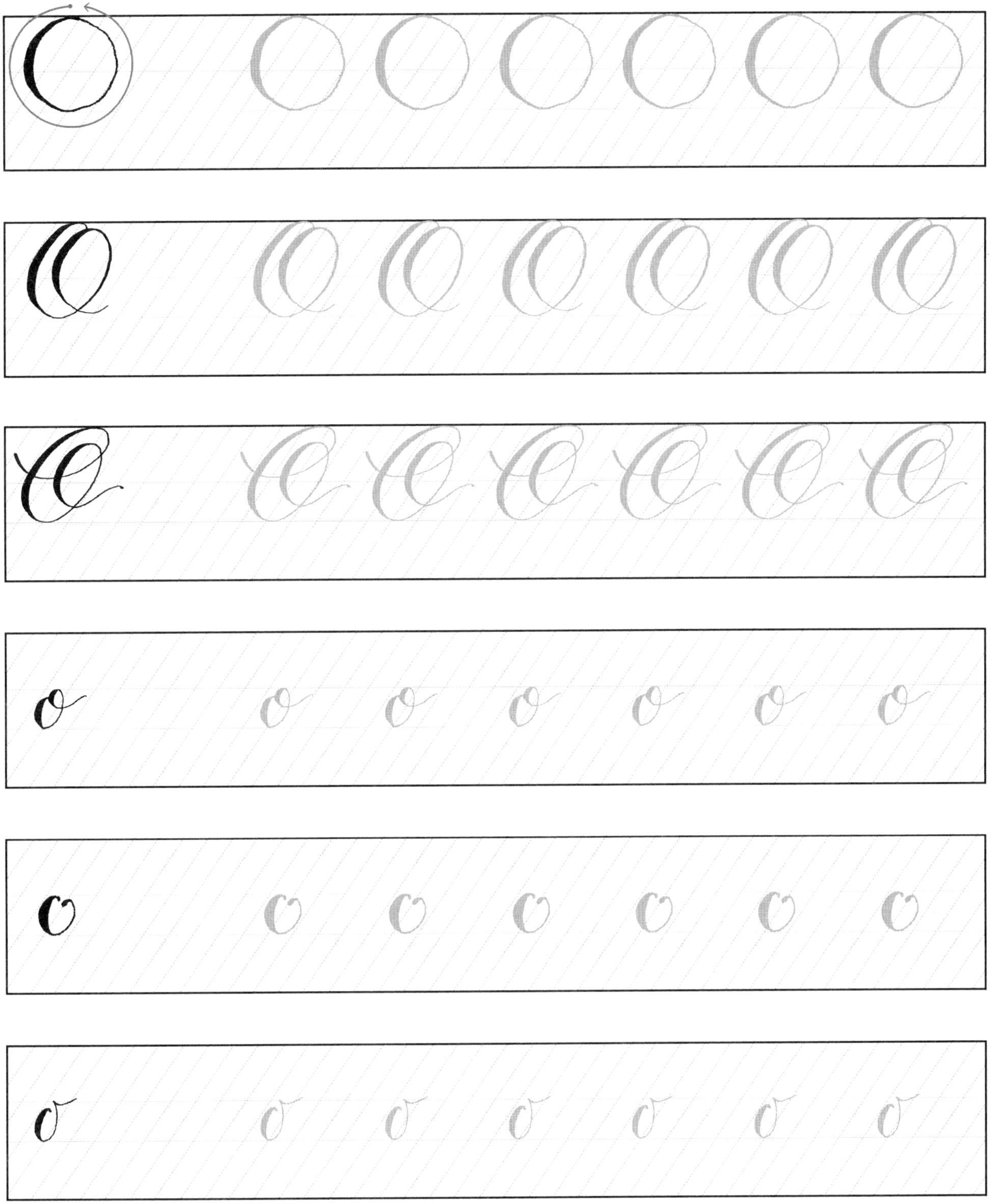

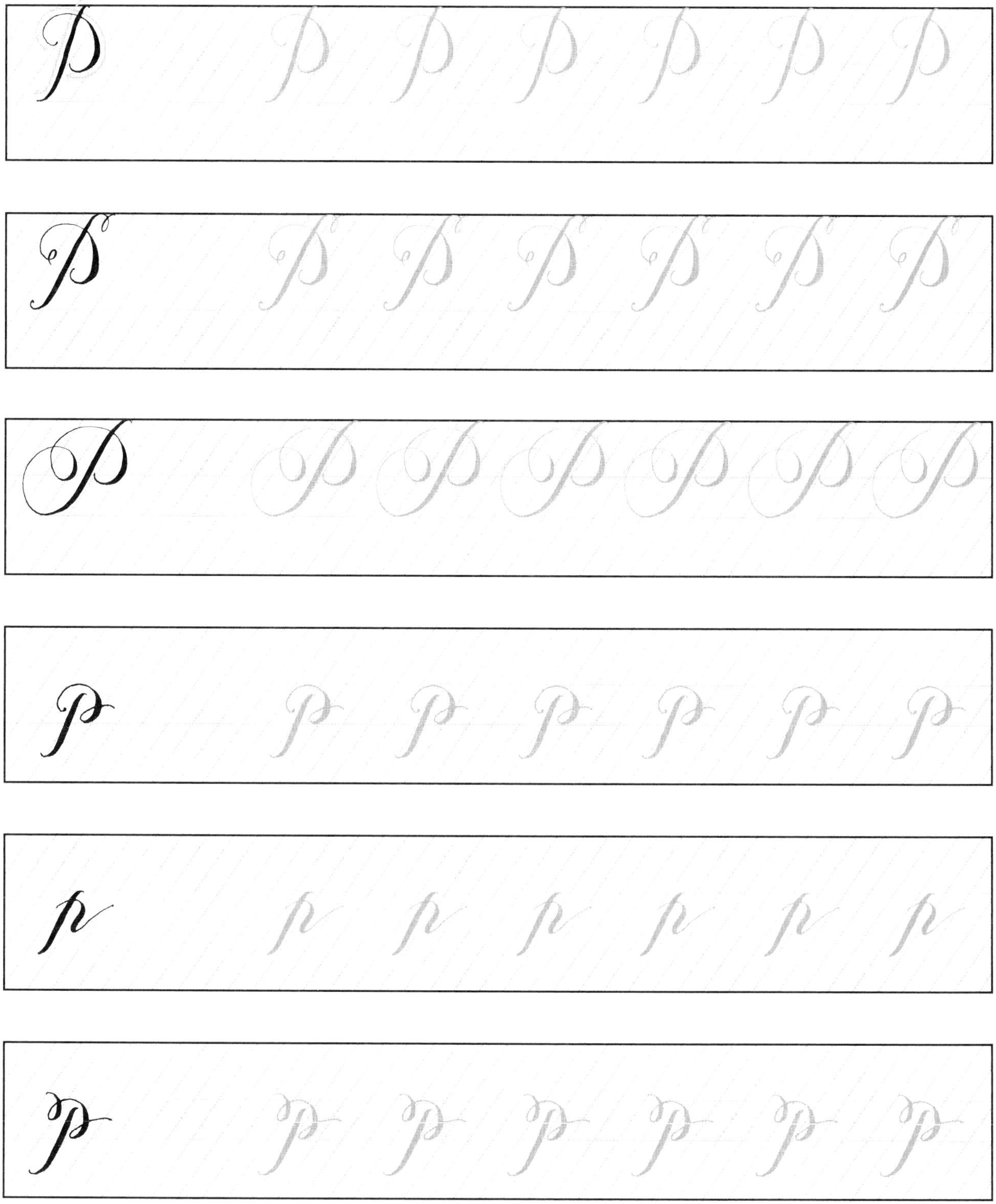

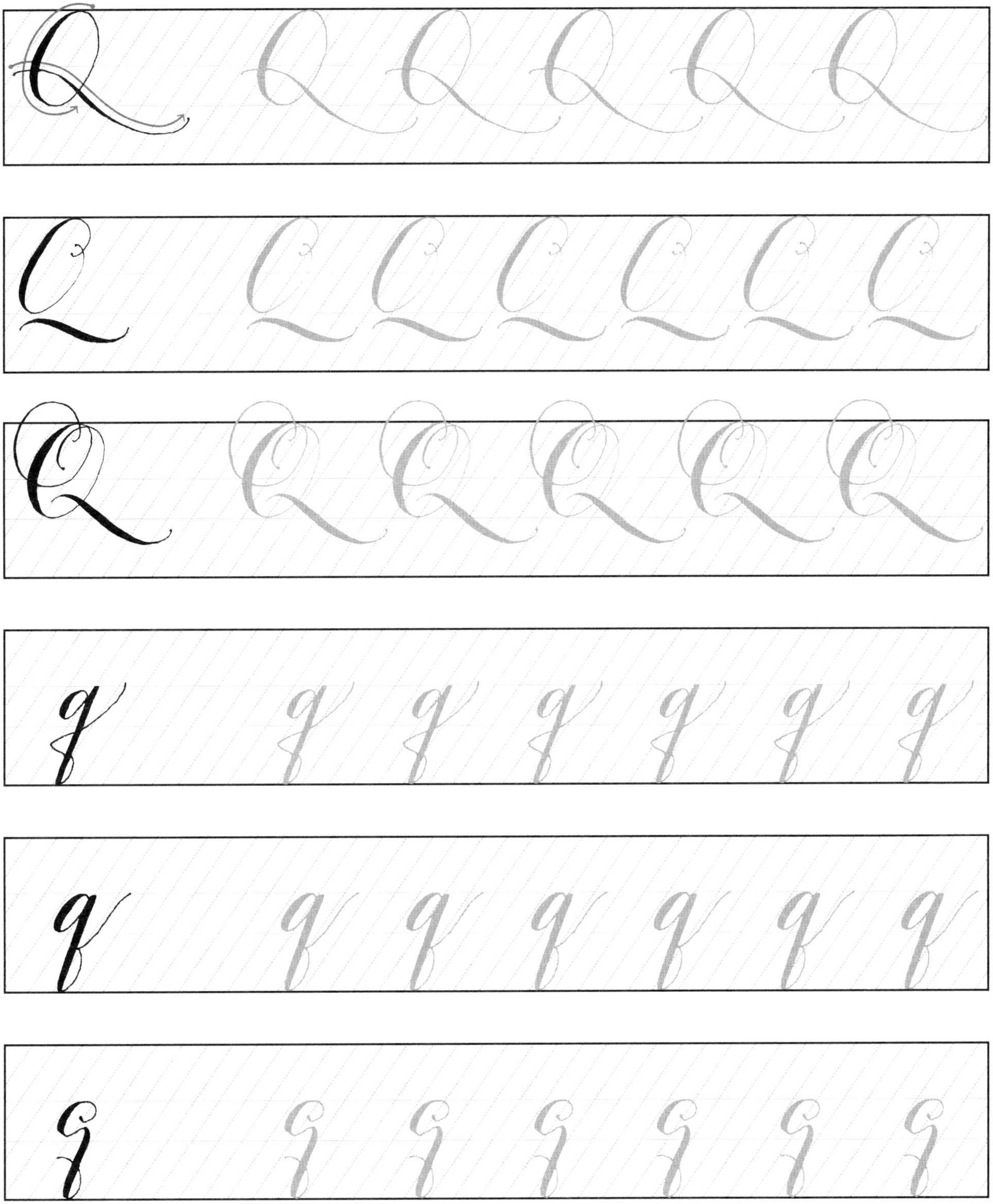

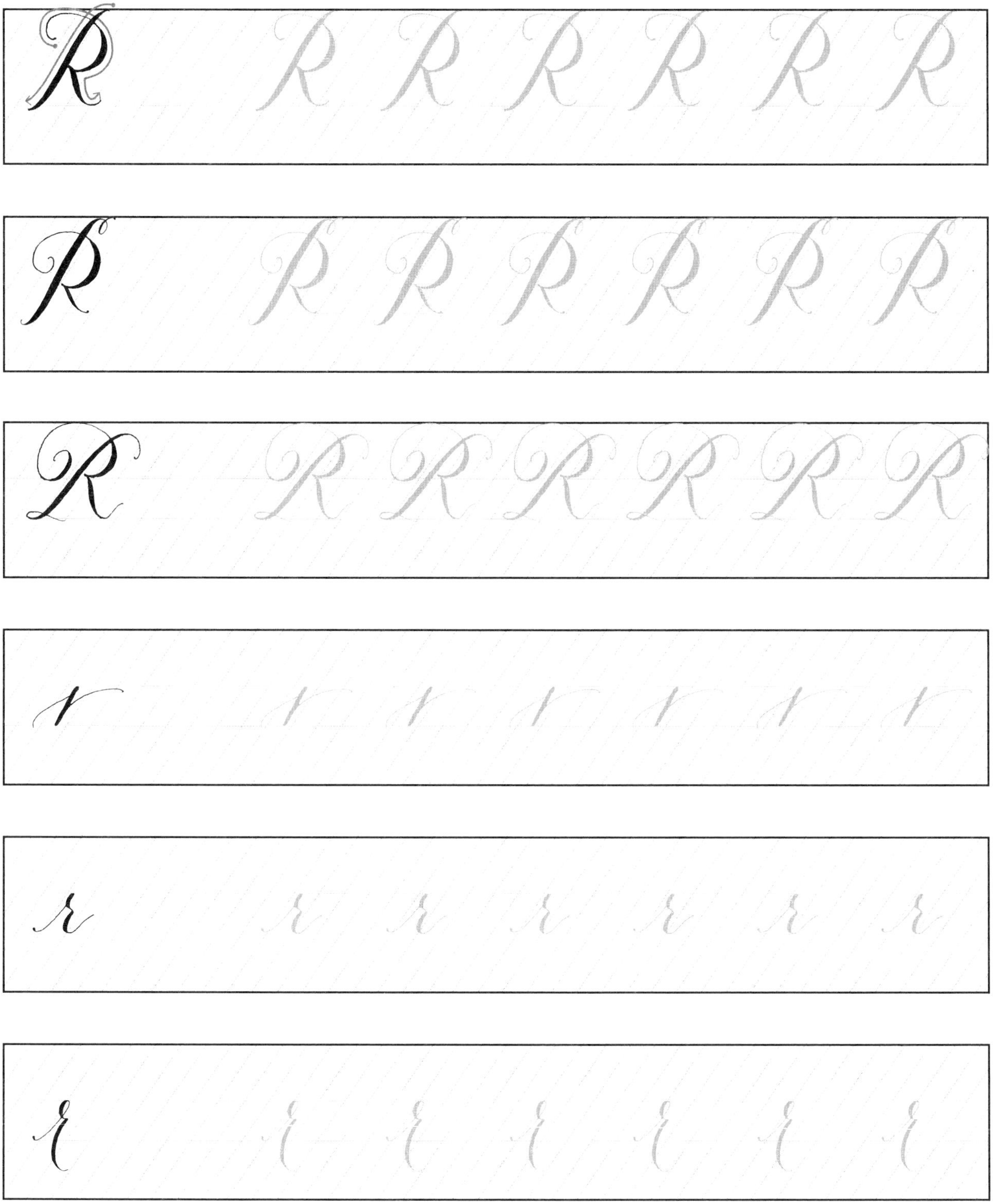

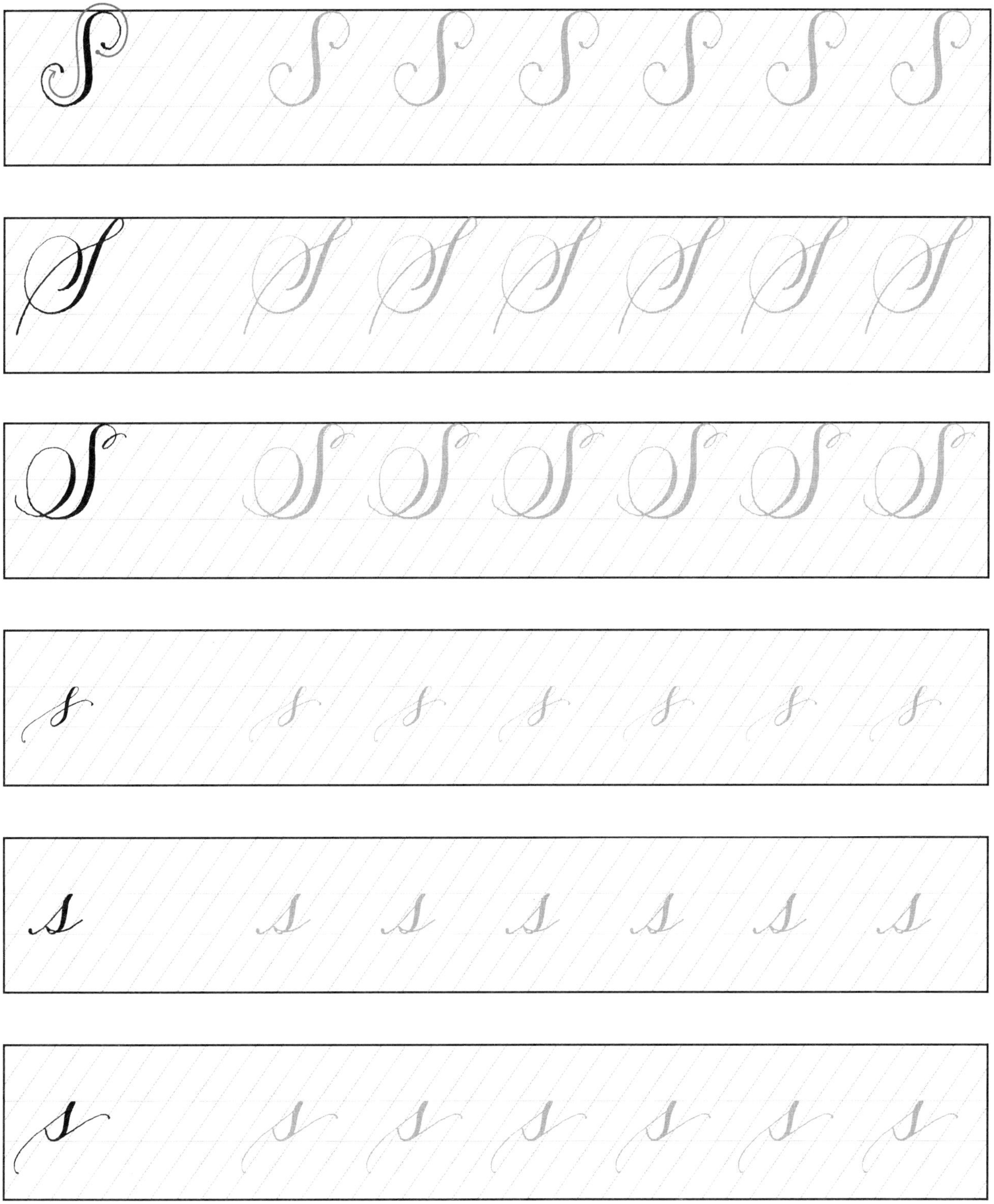

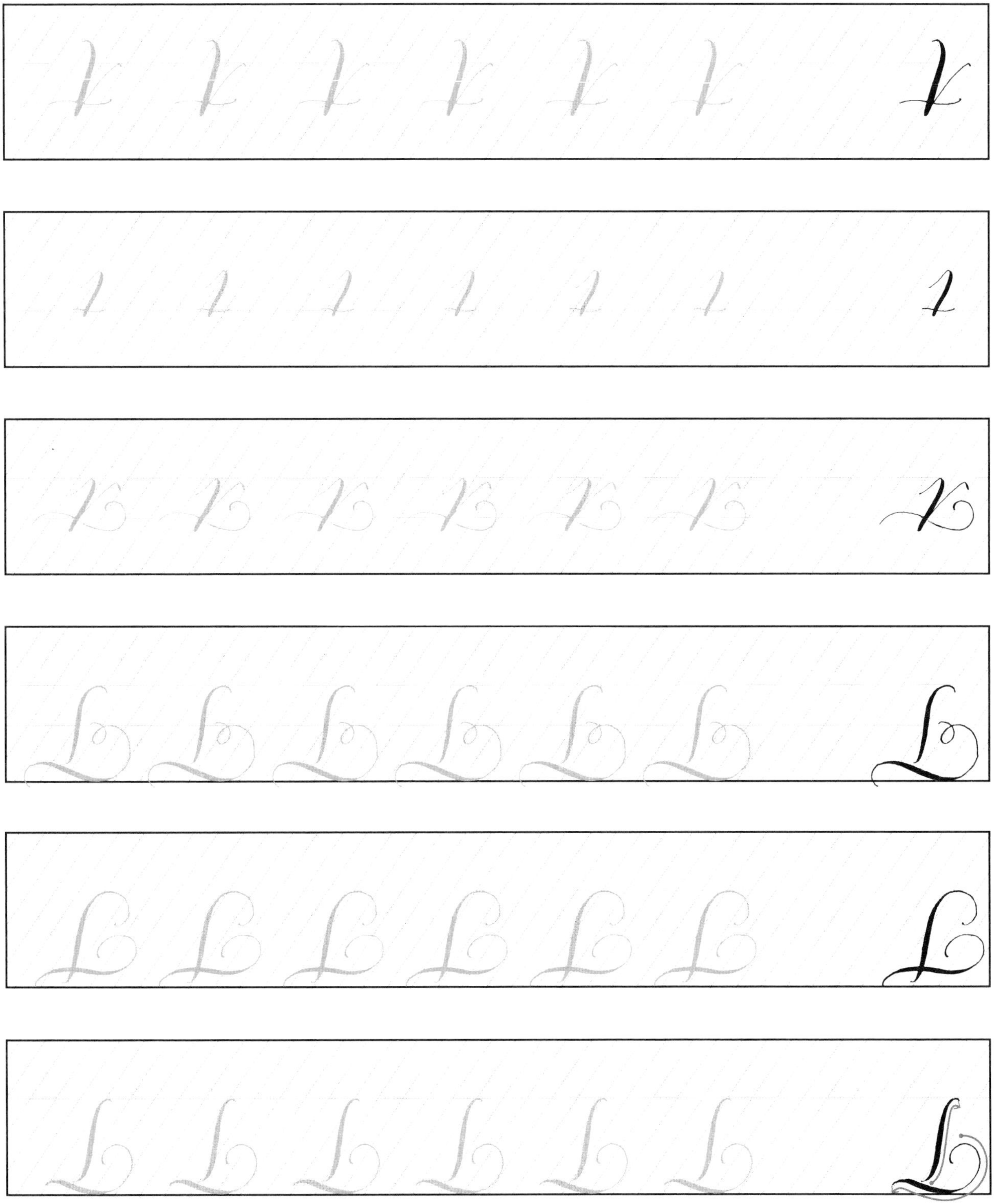

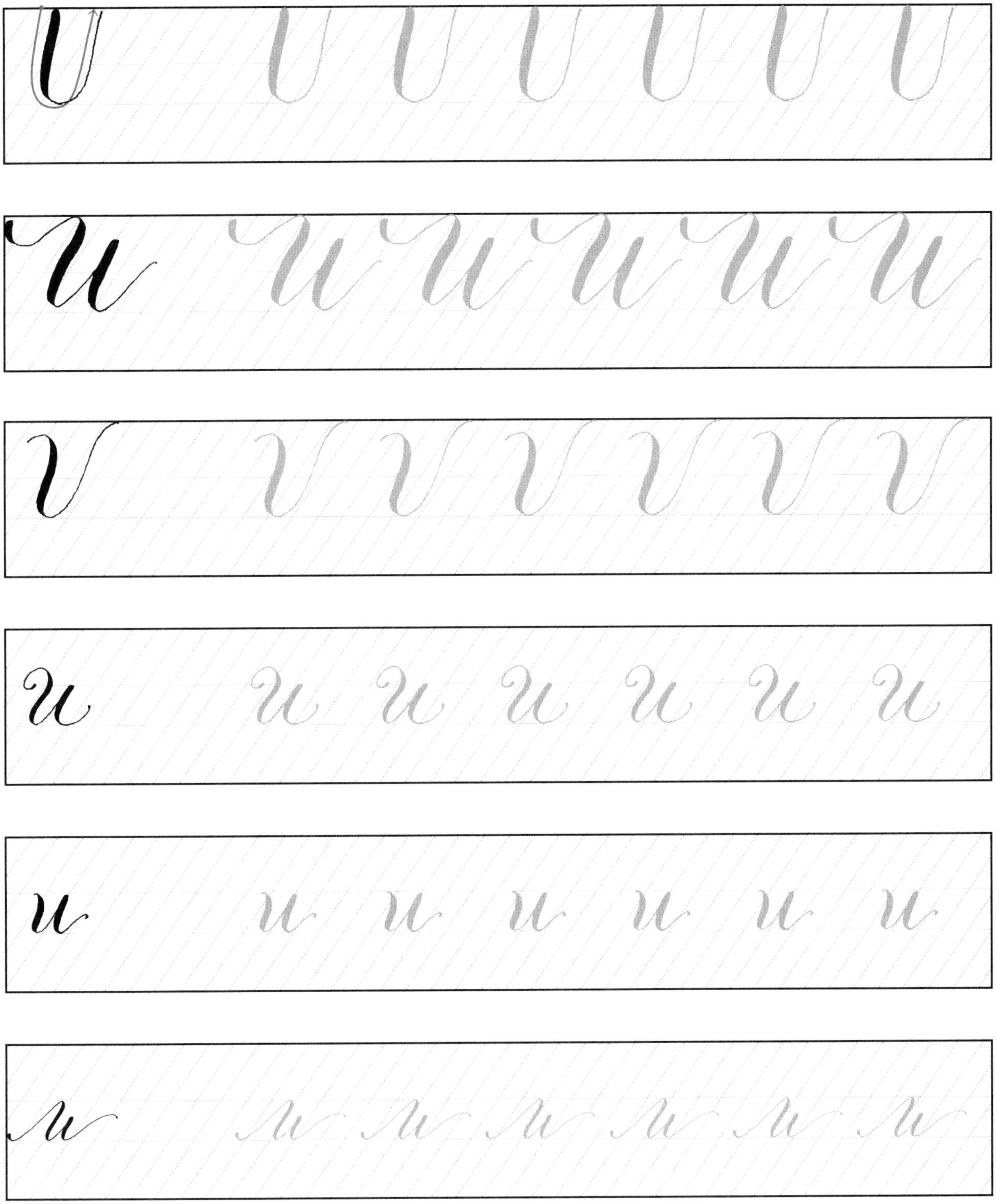

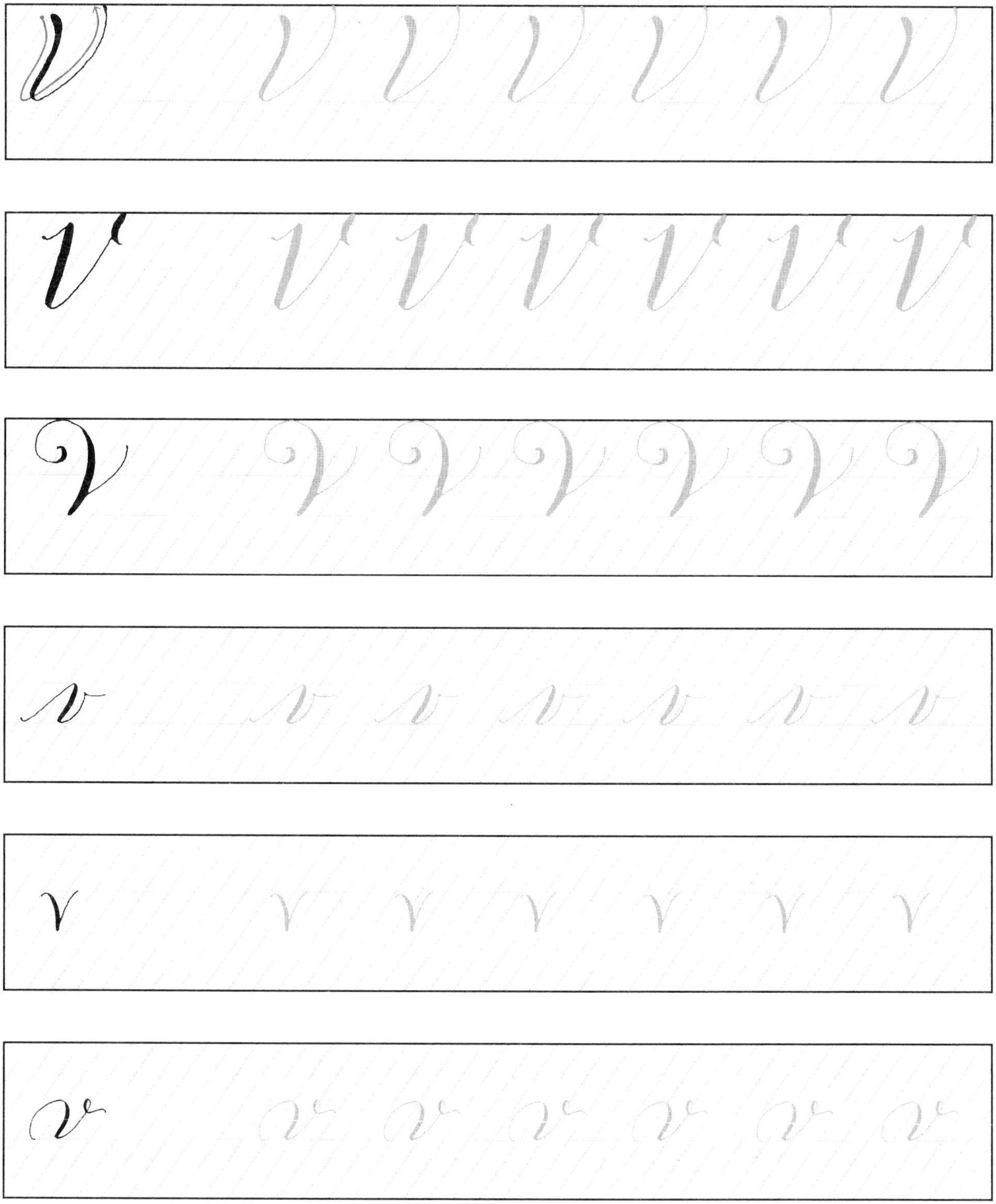

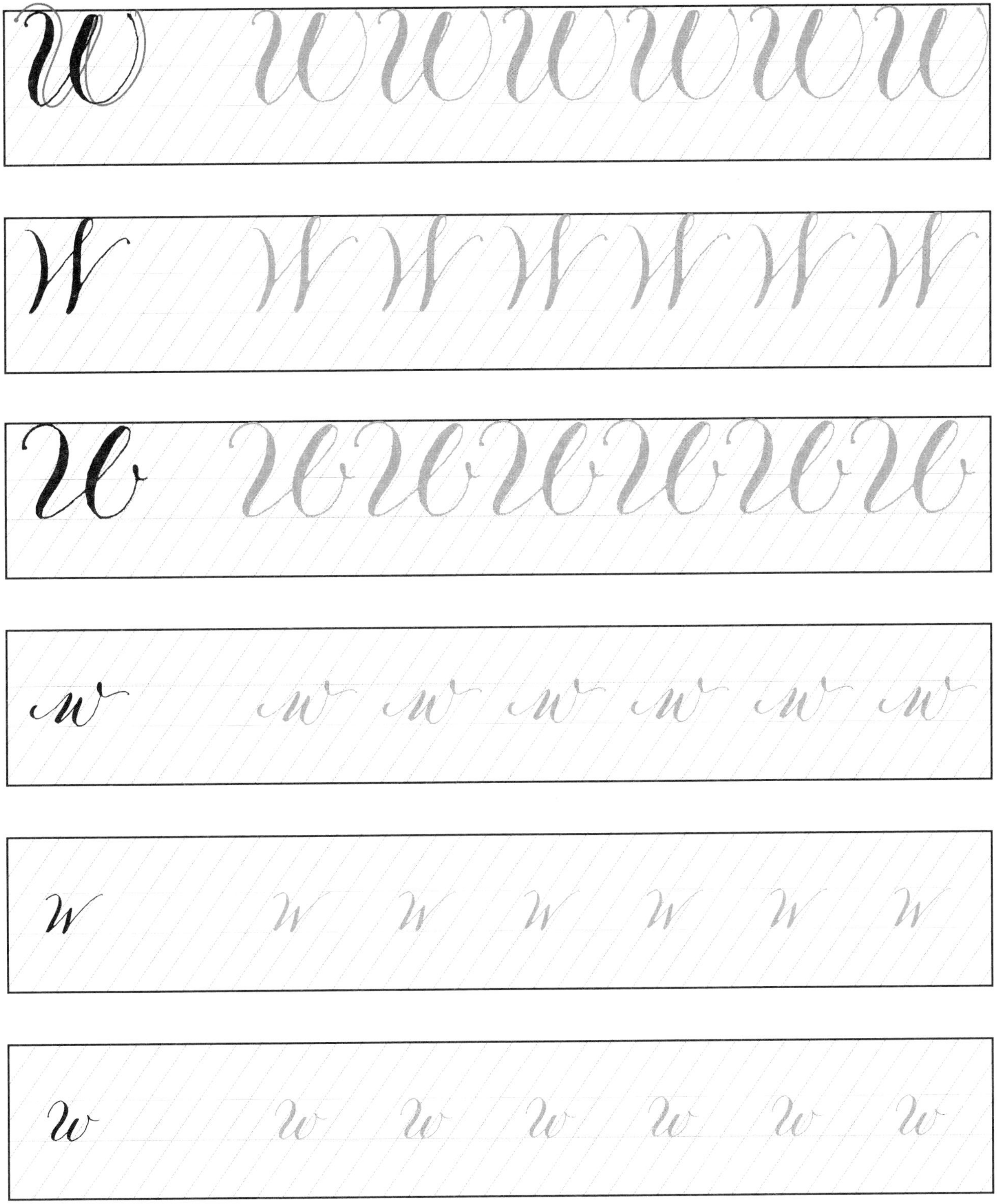

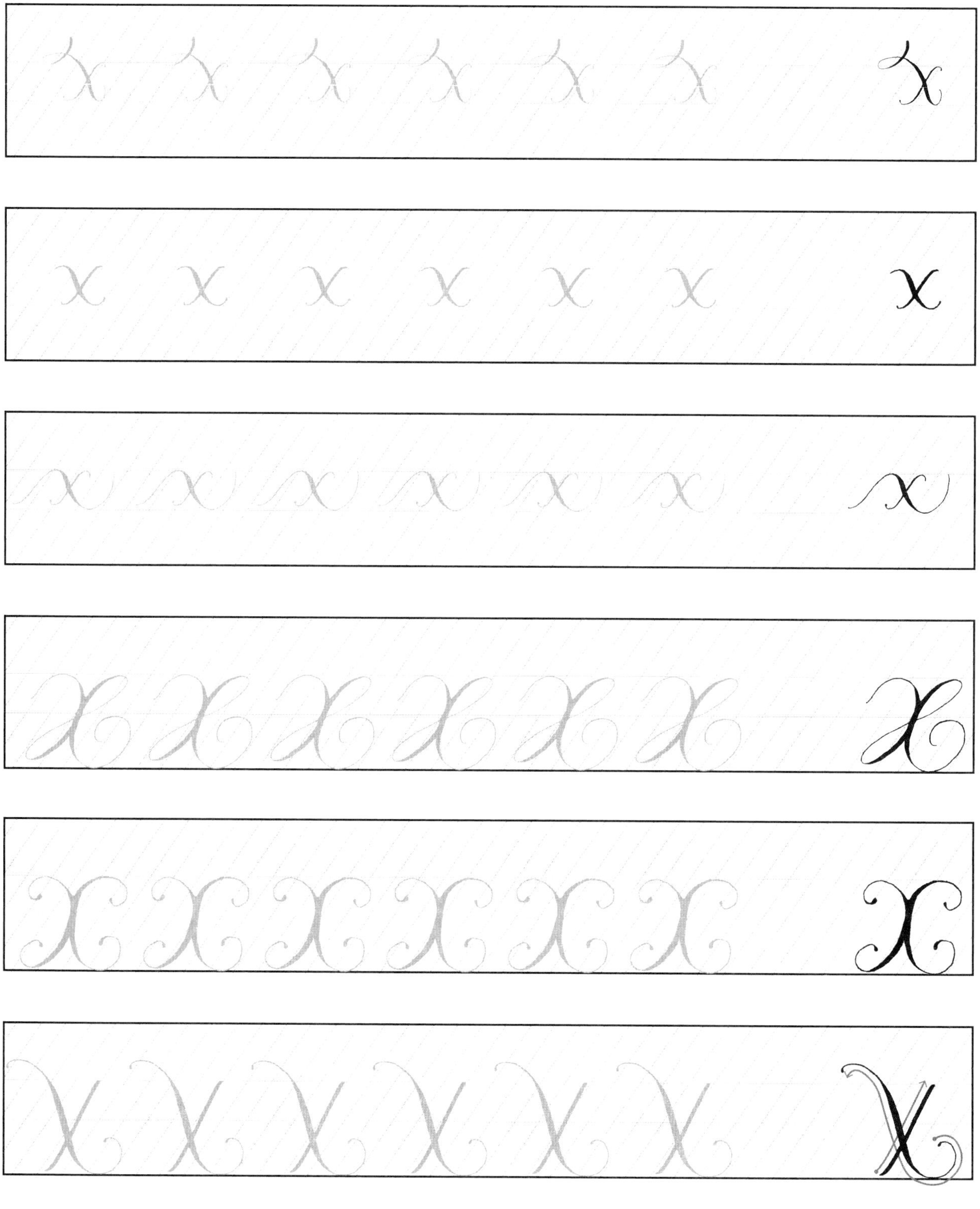

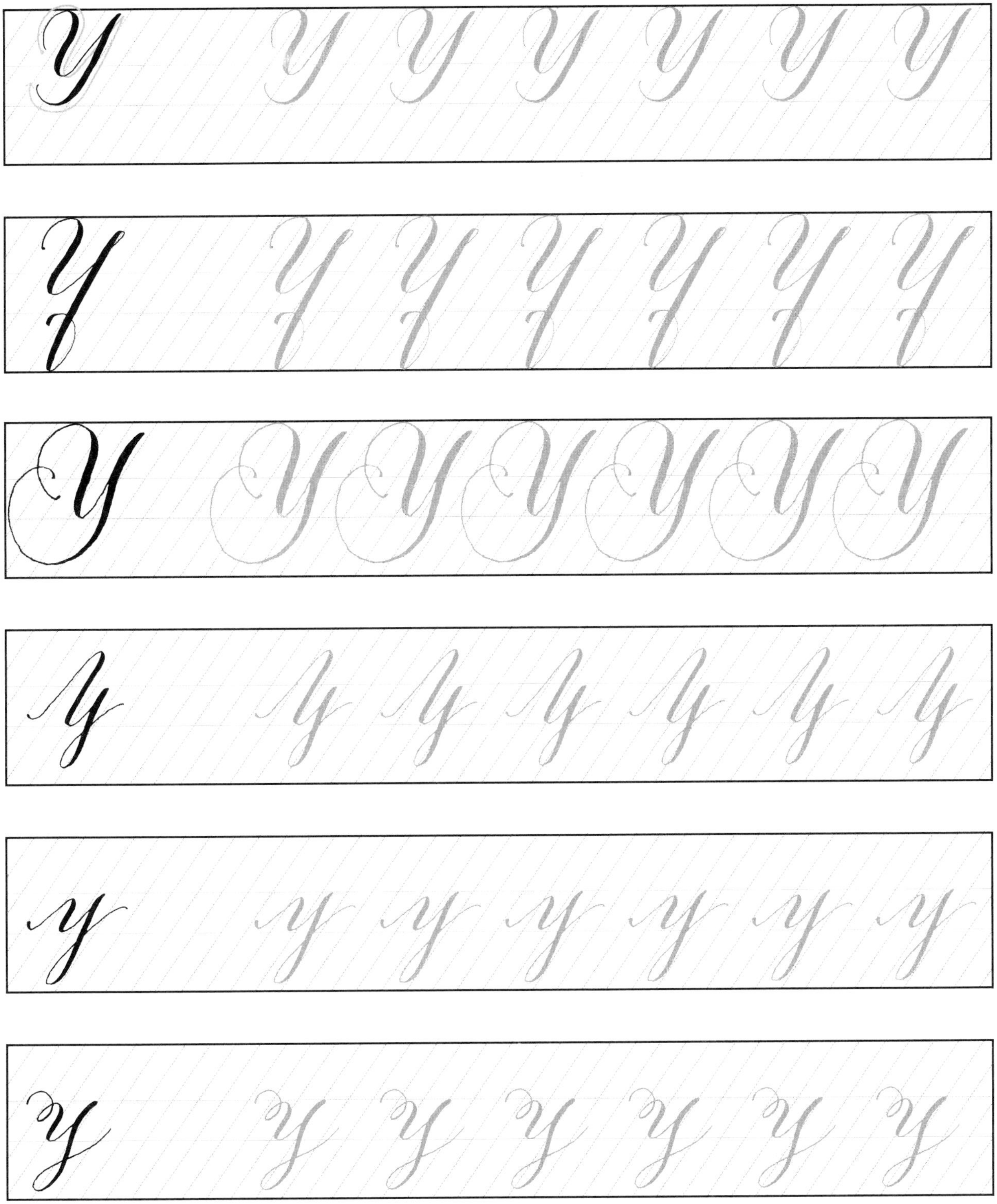

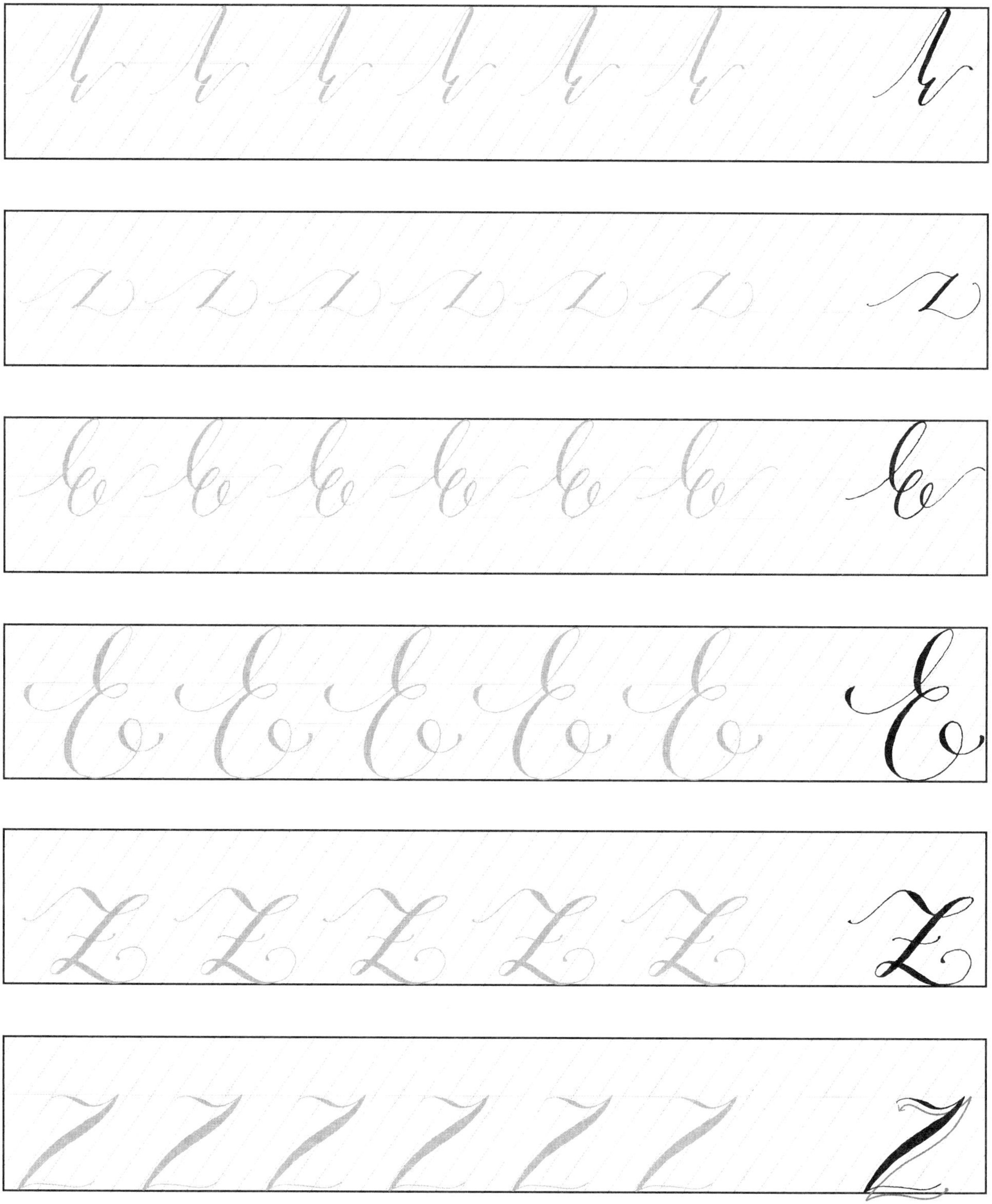

永	永	永	永	永
永	永	永	永	永
永	永	永	永	永
永	永	永	永	永
永	永	永	永	永

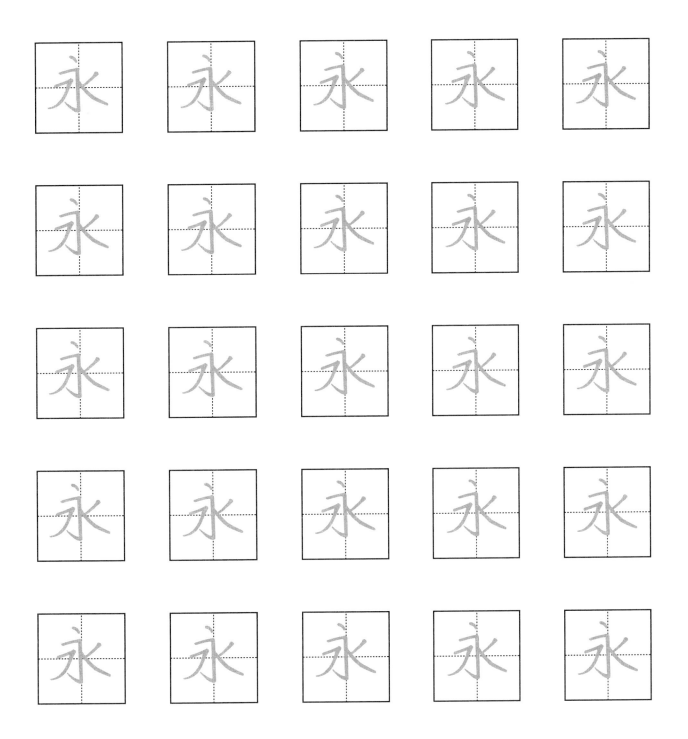

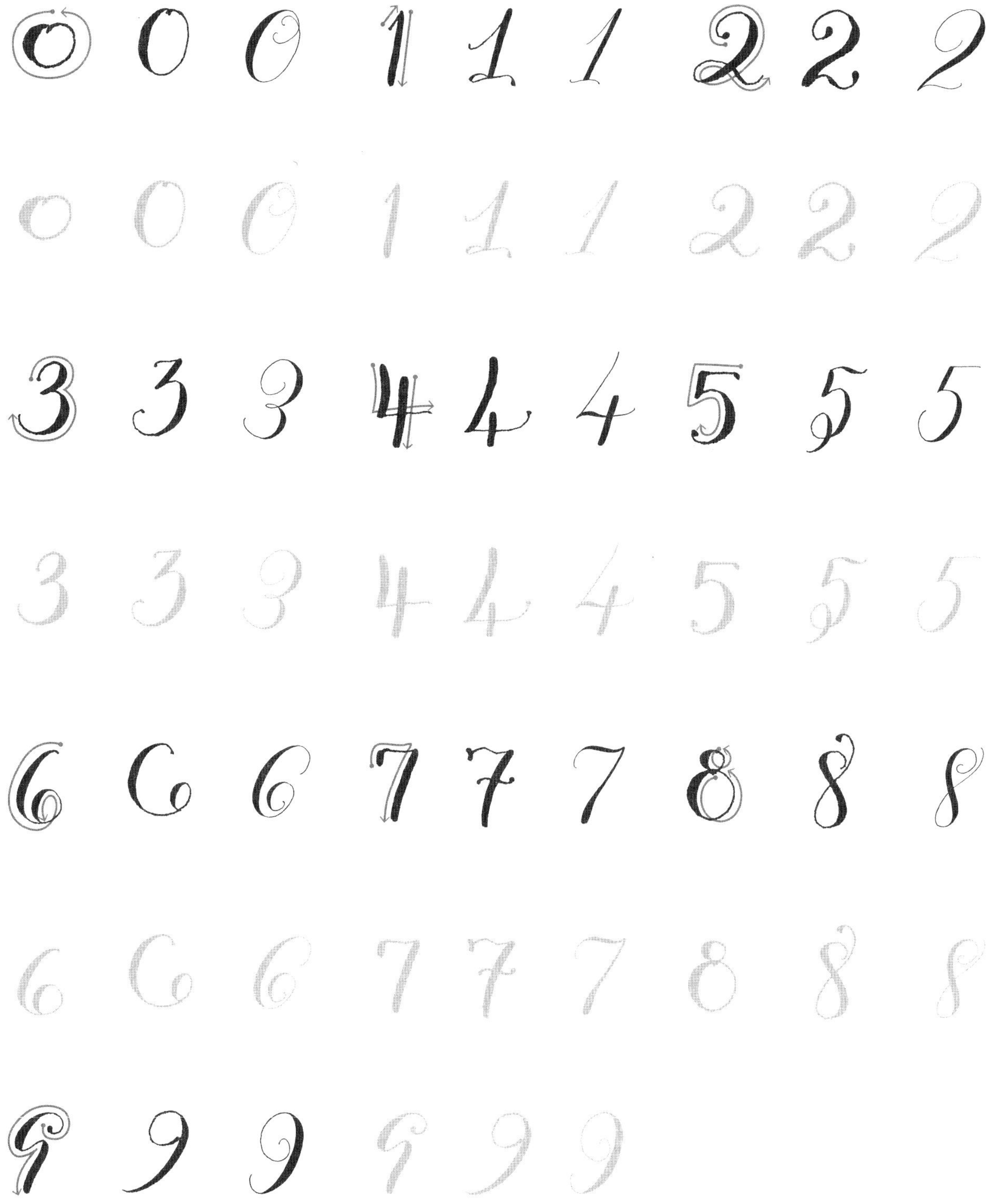

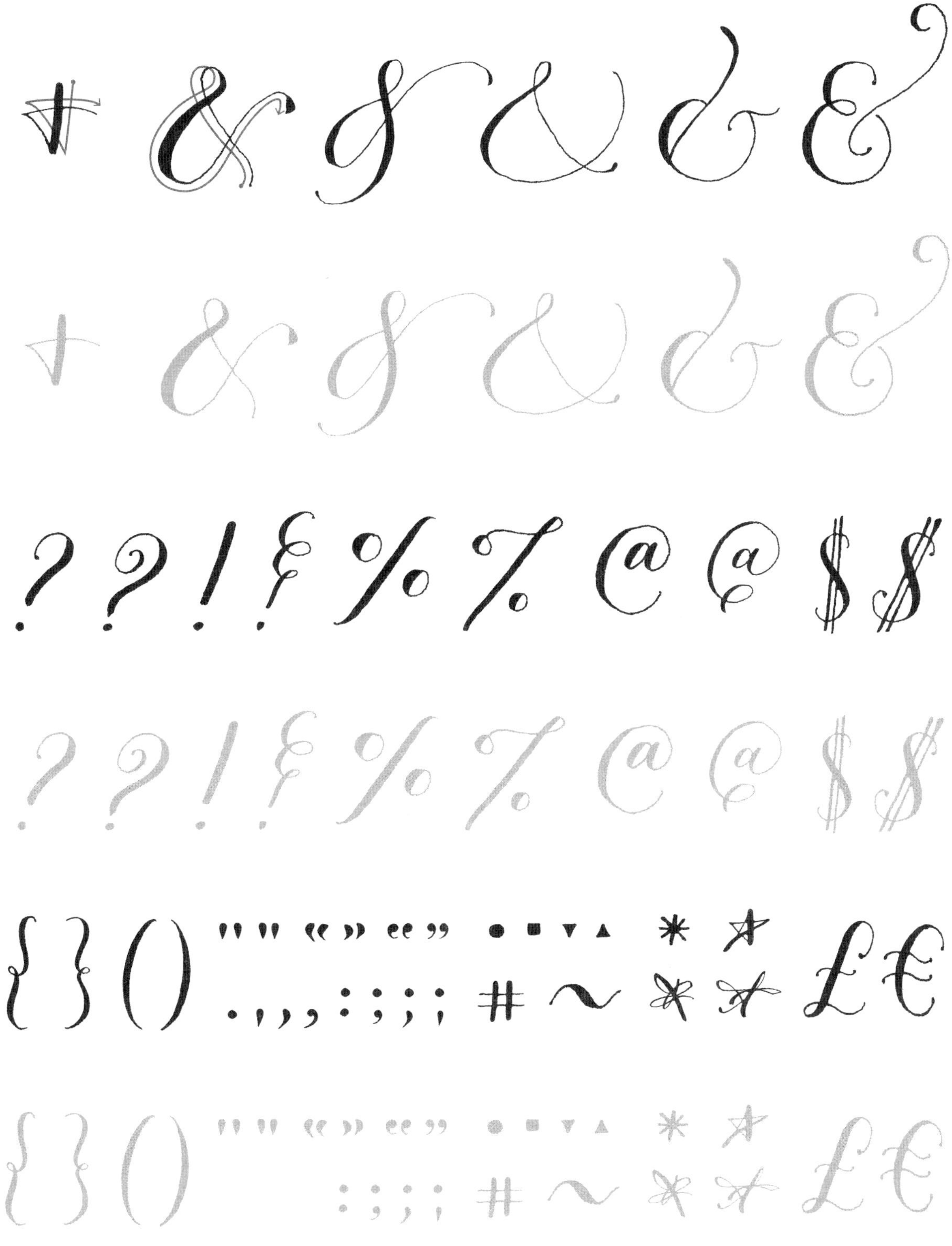

The mystery of love

is

greater than

the mystery of death.

By Oscar Wilde

I can no more, bathed in your langours, O waves,

Sail in the wake of the carriers of cottons,

Nor undergo the pride of the flags and pennants,

Nor pull past the horrible eyes of the hulks.

The Drunken Boat

By Arthur Rimbaud

When you are old and grey and full of sleep,
And nodding by the fire, take down this book,
And slowly read, and dream of the soft look
Your eyes had once, and of their shadows deep;

How many loved your moments of glad grace,
And loved your beauty with love false or true,
But one man loved the pilgrim soul in you,
And loved the sorrows of your changing face;

And bending down beside the glowing bars,
Murmur, a little sadly, how Love fled
And paced upon the mountains overhead
And hid his face amid a crowd of stars.

When You Are Old

By William Butler Yeats

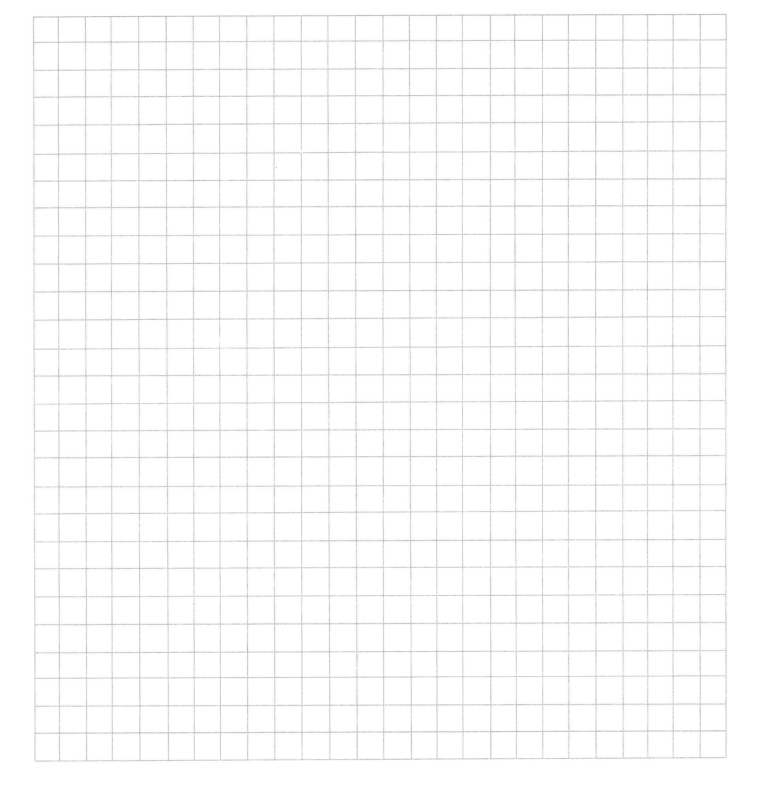

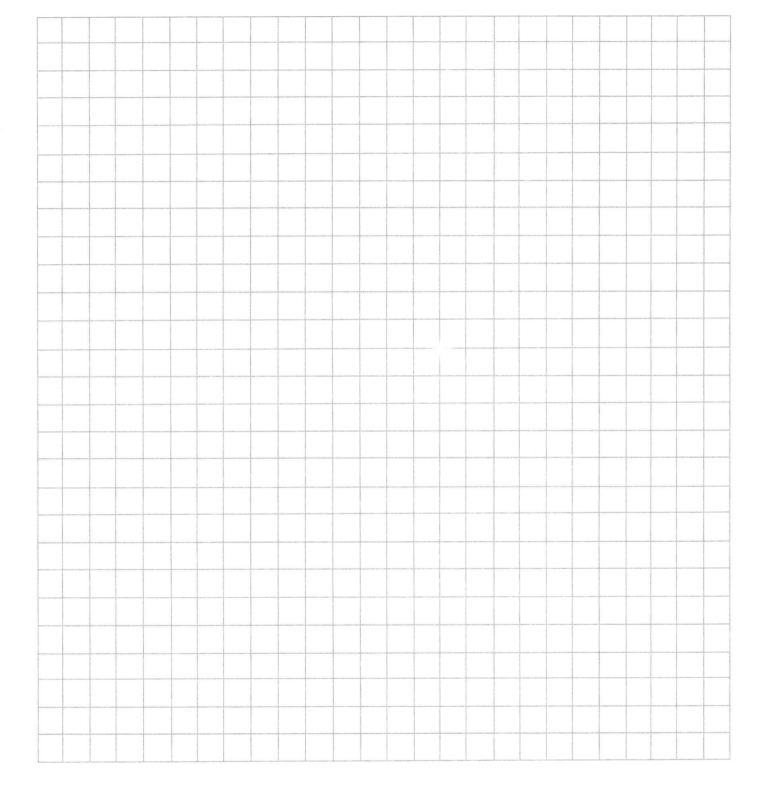

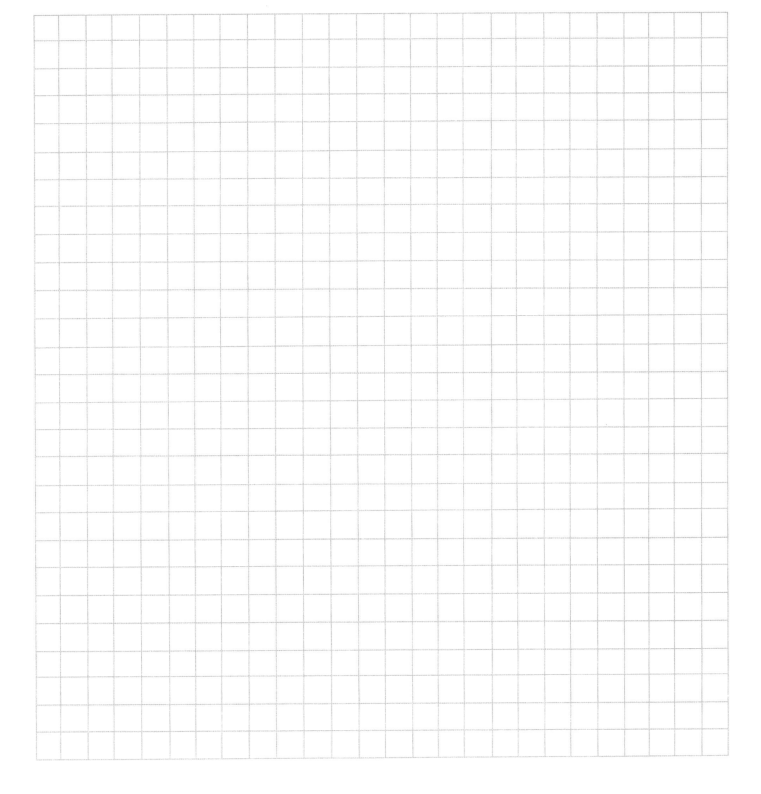

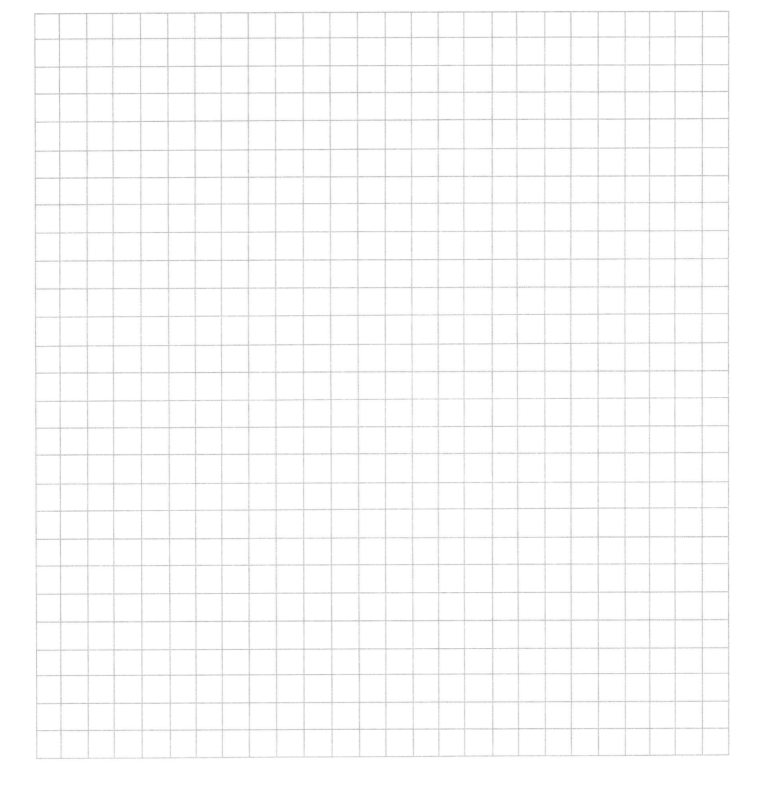

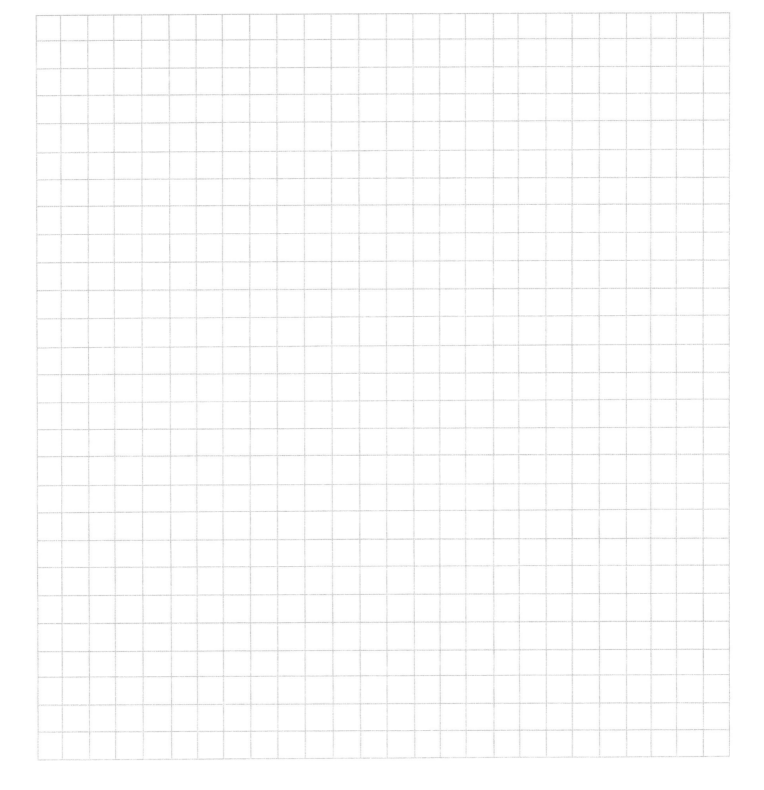

筆尖美學 CALLIGRAPHY

習字簿

筆尖美學
沾水筆英文書法、摩登字體的第一本書

作者 / 莫莉蘇伯索普
主編 / 簡玉芬
責任編輯 / 石文穎
出版者 / 世潮出版有限公司
發行人 / 簡玉芬
地址 / （231）新北市新店區民生路19號5樓
電話 / （02）2218-3277
傳真 / （02）2218-3239（訂書專線）
世茂官網 / www.coolbooks.com.tw
排版製版 / 辰皓國際出版製作有限公司
定價 / 300元

Printed in Taiwan